WILD FLOWERS

BOB GIBBONS

CHANCELLOR
PRESS

This guide covers over 200 species of wild flower, most of which are likely to be found in the UK. In the identification pages (44–125) they are listed broadly by family, although oomo unrelated species may be grouped together. The text gives the common English name, the scentific name in italics, the average height (H – in centimetres), and other useful information on, for example, the type of flower and leaf arrangements. Additional information is given at the end of each dcsoription, in abbreviated form. Fl 4–6 shows the flowering time, with the numbers 1–12 corresponding to the months of the year (eg. 4 = April). Usual habitats are then listed, where H = heathland, Mt = mountainous upland, M = marsh and bog, R = river and lake, C = coastal, F = field and hedgerow, W = wasteland, Wd = woodland, Md = meadow and Pa = pasture. Finally, the type of life-cycle is given – A indicates an annual (a plant that grows from seed, flowers, produces seed and dies, all in one year) B a biennial (a plant that grows from seed in one year, then flowers, produces seed and dies the following year) and P a perennial (a plant that lives on from year to year).

WILD DAFFODIL ▶
Narcissus pseudonarcissus
H 20–35cm. Upright herb, with long, narrow leaves. Flowers have pale yellow petals and golden trumpet. Fl 3–4; Wd, Md, Pa; P.

The author and publishers would like to thank Andrew Branson of British Wildlife Publishing for his assistance in the preparation of this book.

Editor: Julia Gorton
Series designer: Nick Leggett
Designers: Sarah Castell and Mei Lim
Picture researcher: Christine Rista
Production controller: Linda Spillane

First published by Hamlyn,
a division of Octopus Publishing Group Ltd

This edition published in 2000
by Chancellor Press, an imprint of Bounty Books,
a division of Octopus Publishing Group Ltd,
2-4 Heron Quays, London E14 4JP

Printed in Italy

SAFETY CODE

- ALWAYS TELL AN ADULT WHERE YOU ARE GOING, AND WHEN YOU WILL BE BACK
- IF YOU TAKE A DOG WITH YOU, MAKE SURE IT IS ON A LEAD
- TREAT THE COUNTRYSIDE, AND ITS WILDLIFE, WITH RESPECT
- SOME PLANTS ARE EXTREMELY POISONOUS – HANDLE ALL PLANTS WITH CARE, AND NEVER EAT THE BERRIES, LEAVES OR ROOTS OF ANY PLANT UNLESS YOU ARE SURE THAT IT IS SAFE TO DO SO
- DO NOT DRINK WATER FROM A RIVER OR POND

CONTENTS

THE ANATOMY OF PLANTS

An illustration of the important parts of a typical plant – in this case, common chickweed – when in flower.

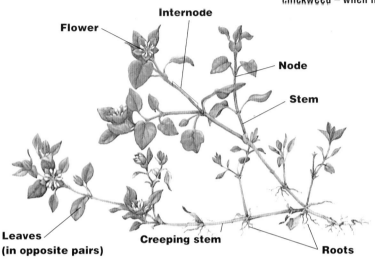

Internode

Flower

Node

Stem

Leaves (in opposite pairs)

Creeping stem

Roots

Over 2,000 species of flowering plant occur throughout Britain and northwest Europe. Some, like the daffodil and daisy, are familiar and instantly recognisable – others may require close examination with a hand lens to distinguish them from other, similar looking species. To be able to identify plants accurately, it is useful to know a little about their different parts and how those parts are named. The four basic features of plants are roots, stems, leaves and flowers. However, the characteristics of each of these features vary enormously between species. For example, plant roots vary from basic, branched, root systems to thick, spreading, food storage organs called tubers. To try to simplify the descriptions of such features, botanists tend to give names to recognisable types of differences. It is worth getting to know a few basic definitions to save looking them up each time.

Some plants have hairs with special glands on them, known as glandular hairs, which may produce scent or some other substance. Glandular hairs are usually easily recognised by their thickened tips, such as these on corn sow-thistle.

Leaf arrangements 1 ▷
The shapes of plant leaves vary considerably. The edges of leaves may be smooth or jagged. The leaf blades may be undivided (simple), or they may be divided (lobed) in various ways. Some leaves may be made up of separate leaflets (compound). The commonest types of leaf shape are shown here.

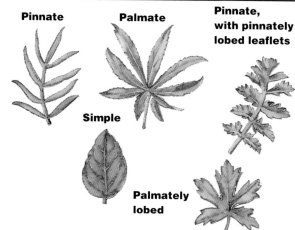

Pinnate

Palmate

Pinnate, with pinnately lobed leaflets

Simple

Palmately lobed

Leaf arrangements 2
The leaves themselves may be arranged on the plant in different ways, and this is usually standard for any given type of plant. A leaf arrangement which has single leaves at each level is called alternate. Leaves arranged in pairs are known as opposite. Opposite leaves may all face the same way, or each pair may be at right angles to the pair below.

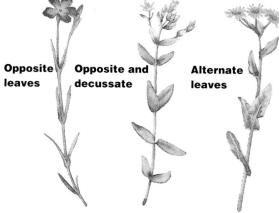

Opposite leaves

Opposite and decussate

Alternate leaves

Leaf arrangements 3 ▷
Some plants have all their leaves in a ring at the base of the stem. This is known as a rosette, and may be combined with some other arrangement. Rings of leaves on the stem are known as whorls. The leaves themselves may be attached to the stem in different ways. They may be stalked or stalkless, clasping the stem tightly or actually growing right around the stem, as on yellow wort.

Whorls of leaves

Rosette of leaves

Perfoliate leaves (yellow wort)

FLOWERS AND FRUIT

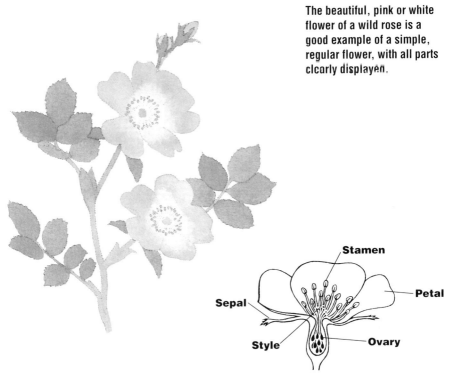

The beautiful, pink or white flower of a wild rose is a good example of a simple, regular flower, with all parts clearly displayed.

Stamen

Petal

Sepal

Style

Ovary

FLOWERS

Flowers vary enormously in size, shape and colour, but they generally have the same basic parts. An outer ring of usually green sepals encircles an inner ring of more colourful petals. There are then a very variable number of stamens, each with a stalk (filament) and a head (anther). The stamens produce the pollen – tiny, dust-like grains which contain the male sex cells. Finally, in the centre of the flower, are the ovaries, containing the female sex cells. On top of each ovary is a style, with a stigma for receiving the pollen. It is the ovaries which will eventually develop into fruits which contain seeds, from which the next generation of plants grow. Sometimes, as in nettles for example, male and female parts are in separate flowers.

The flower of a wild rose eventually develops into a fruit known as a hip. Notice how the hips of this species are crowned with the withered sepals of the original flowers.

6

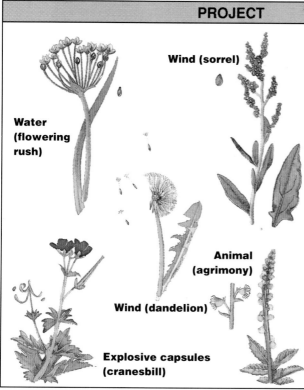

Water (flowering rush)

Wind (sorrel)

Animal (agrimony)

Wind (dandelion)

Explosive capsules (cranesbill)

Plants need to have ways of spreading their seeds to new places. This is especially important for annual plants which die after producing seed, since the site that they grew on may not be suitable for their seeds in the following year. Various ways of spreading, or dispersing, seeds have been developed, depending on the plant's lifestyle, where it grows and what animals are present to help. Some common ways of seed dispersal are shown here. In late summer and autumn, take a look at a variety of plants in seed, and try to work out how their seeds are going to disperse.

Flower arrangements ▷ Flowers are produced in many different arrangements on different plants. Solitary flowers are borne singly, with one flower per stem; other arrangements are much more complex. A group of flowers together on one plant is called an inflorescence. The patterns of branching of the flowers in an inflorescence tend to be the same for a given type of plant. As with the various leaf arrangements, the commonest flower arrangements have been given names by botanists to save describing them in full each time.

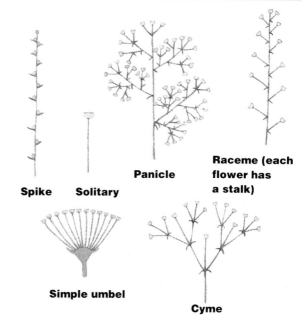

Spike   **Solitary**

Panicle

Raceme (each flower has a stalk)

Simple umbel

Cyme

POLLINATION

The flowers of white dead-
nettle are highly attractive to
bees, which move from
flower to flower collecting
pollen.

Pollination is the process of transferring pollen
from stamen to stigma. It is possible for flowers
to pollinate themselves, or other flowers on the
same plant (self-pollination). It is, however,
much better for the health of the species if cross-
pollination occurs ie. pollen is transferred from
one plant to another. Plants have developed
various mechanisms to transfer pollen amongst
themselves. The most common method involves
the insects that are attracted to the flowers for
their nectar. Pollen grains stuck to the insects'
bodies are effectively transferred from one plant
to another as the insect moves from flower to
flower. Other types of flower, usually less
colourful, use wind to transport their pollen.

Stigma

Style

Ovary

Anther

Stamen

Filament

A closer view of a stamen,
style, stigma and ovary of a
flower. Pollen grains stick to
the stigma before growing
into the ovary.

The flowers of orchids are highly specialised for pollination by insects. Within the flowers of most species, the single male anther, with its two pollen masses on stalks – called pollinia – are situated above the female stigma. When the insect pushes into the flower to reach the nectar, the pollinia stick onto its head. But they do not come into contact with the stigma of the same flower, as the bee feasts on the nectar, because the pollinia are held out of the way by their stalks. However, after a short time (and almost certainly when the insect has moved onto another flower), the pollinia bend forwards. They are then perfectly positioned to pollinate the stigma of the next orchid flower visited.

Insect visits first flower

Pollinia gradually bend forward

Insect pollinates flowers on nearby plant

PROJECT

You can quite easily observe the remarkable movement of an orchid's pollinia, as described above. Choose a spike of a marsh, spotted or early purple orchid with plenty of open flowers. Carefully extract a pollinium by inserting the point of a sharp pencil or similar object into the 'mouth' of a flower. Notice how, when you withdraw the pencil, the pollinium is held erect on its stalk. Watch closely, and within a couple of minutes it will bend miraculously forwards, almost to a horizontal position.

Position of pollinia when removed from flower

Position after 1–2 minutes

EQUIPMENT

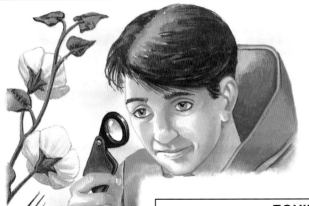

◀ A small hand lens such as this is very useful for examining some of the small, distinguishing features of plants. A magnification of x8 or x10 is best. When viewing, place the lens to the eye, then move close to the plant. Make sure that you position yourself so that you have as much light as possible.

▲ If you are going on a serious plant-hunting expedition, bear in mind the conditions you are going to encounter. In mountain areas, you will always need to take extra clothing, because it can be much colder on mountain tops than in the valleys below. Boots or strong trainers are best for long days out.

EQUIPMENT

The equipment that you really need to be a field botanist is very limited and generally cheap. A hand lens, as above, is very important. In addition, you need a good book or two to help with identification. You may be lucky enough to find information on local 'flora' – the types of flowering plants that occur in your area – at your library. A hard-backed notebook and pencil, or waterproof pen, together with some polythene bags and a map, complete the essential kit. A camera and a pair of binoculars are useful, but they are certainly not necessary at first.

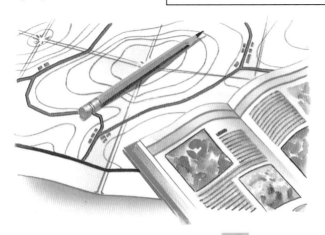

◀ Good books on plants are essential for learning more about them. Wherever possible, take the books out with you so that you can look at the book and the flowers together. A large scale map of your chosen area (at least 1:50,000 scale), will make location-finding easier, and will enable you to pick out some interesting habitats.

It is a good idea to keep ▷ records of the flowers you see. Transfer field notes from your book onto cards, which you can write out neatly. If appropriate, add a photograph too. Keep details of locations, flowering dates, and any other information of interest. Classify the cards in alphabetical or family order, perhaps in a shoe box or other suitable container.

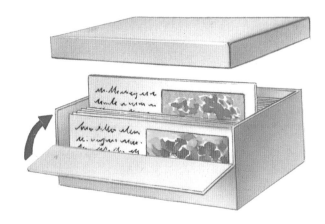

RECORDING

You might think that everything there is to know about flowers and their distribution – where different species grow – is already known. In actual fact, records are not complete, and there is still a great deal more to be discovered. Even a beginner may, in the course of field studies, observe and record something unique, so it is essential to keep detailed and accurate records of all that you find. If you do come across something that seems very unusual, tell a knowledgeable local botanist about your discovery. He or she may well want to come and check it with you.

If you want to make a good ▽ photographic record of a particular location, but find it difficult to fit it all into one frame, then try taking a series of photos from one point and making a montage with them afterwards.

◁ Taking photographs of the flowers you see is a good way to keep souvenirs of your trips without having to pick anything. Because most flowers are quite small, you really need a camera that focuses close to the subject. The best camera to use is a Single Lens Reflex (SLR), because you view and photograph through the same lens, making accurate close-ups very easy.

HOW TO LOOK

HOW TO LOOK

The key to finding and enjoying flowers lies in being able to look successfully. Rather than trying to identify something quickly, and then moving onto the next flower, it is worth looking carefully at what you have and making sure you know exactly what it is. Look closely at all the significant parts – are the leaves toothed or not? – how are the leaves arranged on the stem? – does the flower have purple veins, or is it plain? – and so on. In this way, you will soon learn about the structure of flowers and flowering plants, as well as getting to know the typical characteristics of some of the main plant families. As you build up your knowledge, identification becomes easier and easier.

Use your hand lens to check out any small details. Are there glandular hairs on the flowers? Does the stigma really split into four lobes, or is there only one? These details may sound small, but they are part of the way in which flowers are distinguished from each other, and you often need a lens to see them. While you are looking at anything in flower, look carefully at its lower leaves – this helps to recognise the plant if you see it again when it is not in flower. It is very difficult to identify plants from leaves alone otherwise.

If you cannot identify a plant in the field, you may need to make notes and sketches to help identify it later. Write down details of where the plant is growing, whether it is common or rare, how tall it is, and so on. Make careful drawings of leaf shape and flower characteristics and try to describe the colour of the flower as accurately as you can.

It is also worth making general notes about your field trips. Note the place, date, and habitat type (e.g. heathland). Then, as well as listing the plants you have found, write down other details such as the kind of butterflies seen.

FINDING FLOWERS

Before you can begin to identify flowers, you first need to find them. To learn when and where to look for flowers, you will need to know a little about the life cycles of different plants, and their ecology – the sorts of habitats they can be found in and the types of living things they are likely to be found with.

Hilly woodland
Old woods of deciduous (leaf-shedding) trees in hilly areas often have an especially interesting variety of flowers. Visit them in spring and look along paths or in coppiced areas.

Hill pasture
Rough hill pastures are often especially good for flowers, particularly those on chalk or limestone. Generally, the steeper they are the better, since difficult ground cannot be farmed with heavy machinery.

Meadows
Meadows which are cut for hay or silage are usually on better soils than pastures and are more often fertilised or reseeded. Look for colourful ones before they are cut in midsummer, and look again in autumn.

Open water
Open water and the banks that surround it often have many plants of interest. Look in unpolluted still or slow-flowing water, preferably not too deep.

Ditches
Well-managed, unpolluted ditches may have wonderful displays of both common and rare flowers, as well as being good for dragonflies, frogs and other creatures.

Watch out for bulls or over-enthusiastic bullocks along footpaths or in areas where you wish to look. Bulls in fields with footpaths should be safe, by law, but take care not to get carried away looking for flowers and forget where you are.

COUNTRY CODE

- Respect all wildlife

- Keep dogs under control

- Never trespass on private property

- Close all gates

- Don't go near dangerous places, such as pits or steep-sided rivers

- Avoid all risk of fire

- Keep to paths wherever possible, particularly across farmland

- Do not drop litter

- Avoid causing damage to hedges, walls or fences

Grazed pasture
If pasture is level and bright green through being fertilised, its plant life will be dull. But if the pasture is uneven, especially with anthills, or obviously wet in places, then it will be worth taking a look.

Hedgerows
Old hedgerows often have a lovely mixture of woodland and grassland flowers. Look along hedges that border pasture and meadow rather than sprayed arable land.

Field edges
If you look along the rough areas around fields, you may find quite a different selection of plants, since here they are allowed to grow taller.

CONSERVATION

Ponds need clearing out occasionally to maintain their populations of both plants and animals. If neglected, they tend to gradually dry up.

Over the last few decades, very large areas of natural habitats, once rich in plant and animal life, have disappeared under buildings, roads and farms. Modern farming methods, with large fields, intensive use of pesticides, and high crop yields, do not give many wild flowers a chance to grow. Nowadays, most species survive in places where these changes have not taken place – old woodland and heathland, for example. However, natural habitats are still disappearing fast, and constant effort is needed to conserve what is left. Even habitats that are protected from development by law still need management. Otherwise, they may deteriorate so much that they become unsuitable for the species that depend on them for survival.

Many areas of natural habitat are now just isolated 'islands' in a sea of hostile farmland, such as this grassland nature reserve surrounded by fields.

There are hundreds of nature reserves scattered throughout the country. Some are run by the government, while others get their funds from charities dedicated to protecting nature. Usually, nature reserves conserve a whole area of habitat rather than just one or two rare species, and most of them are good places for flowers. Your local library can help with details.

A few plants are now so rare that they have become valuable. Some collectors or dealers attempt to dig up the rarest plants, such as orchids, so that they can sell them. In order to try to stop this, conservation organisations may have to mount 24-hour watches on vulnerable plants, or erect wire cages over especially valuable plants such as monkey orchids or lady's slipper orchids.

Nowadays, more and more people have time to go out into the countryside, yet there are fewer and fewer unspoilt places that they can go to. This means that any especially attractive places, such as these coastal dunes, have vast numbers of visitors, which can disturb, or erode, the soil and cause serious problems for the wildlife. Erosion can destroy plant habitats, and breeding birds and mammals are continually disturbed.

YOUR OWN WILDLIFE GARDEN

As well as being pleasant places for relaxation, gardens can be havens for wildlife. With a little planning and effort, it is possible to turn your garden into a marvellous, miniature nature reserve, which will give you and your visitors endless pleasure and excitement besides helping to conserve wildlife. The layout shown here gives some ideas, although it is only one possibility. It is a good general principle to cut down on pesticides, to help encourage insect-eating birds and a good diversity of insects. Keep the area near the house well-maintained, but let the grass grow a little taller towards the bottom of the garden.

Insect border ▼
In a sheltered, sunny area, plant a border of colourful, nectar-producing flowers. They will attract plenty of butterflies and insects, as well as making a beautiful and aromatic display.

Pond ▶
A good pond is the focal point of a wildlife garden. Dig it so that there are both shallow and deep areas, and have plenty of floating plants as well as those that live at the water's edge.

Rough grass ▼
A small, rough grass area, perhaps with an old tree stump and planted with bulbs, makes a good little area for wildlife and some other types of flowers.

Path ▼
Have a good mown or paved path through your wildlife area. This gives better access and makes it easier to see the various plants and animals.

Lawn ▼
Even a traditional well-mown lawn can be good for wildlife if you allow extra low-growing flowers, such as daisies and speedwell, to flourish and attract insects.

▲ **Long grass**
A long grass area, filled with ox-eye daisies, red clover, vetches, selfheal, cowslips and other flowers, will be like a miniature meadow, very attractive to insects and other creatures.

STRANGE LIVES

Mistletoe lives as a semi-parasite on trees such as apple and poplar. Its seeds are spread by the birds that eat its berries. The berry seeds stick to their beaks, which they then wipe off onto a new tree.

Most flowers get their nutrients from the soil and make food with the help of sunlight and their green colouring (chlorophyll). Some, however, have evolved different ways of surviving. There are, for example, plants that are parasites. They obtain all their food requirements from other plants, and cannot make their own at all e.g. dodder. Then there are semi-parasites, which also take food from other plants, but are able to make some of their own, such as mistletoe, or eyebright. Other plants catch and digest insects to provide them with nutrients that are not available in the acid, boggy places where they live; the sundews, bladderworts and butterworts are examples of insect-eating plants.

Sundews live in boggy areas with poor soil. To ensure a good nutrient supply, their leaves are covered with sticky hairs that can trap any small insect that lands on them. The insect is then slowly digested.

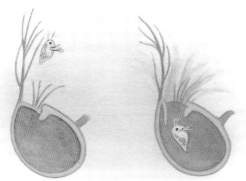

The bladderworts are a small group of water plants that 'eat' insects. They catch their prey underwater, with small bladders on their leaves, each equipped with a little trigger. When the trigger is touched by a small insect, a tiny door opens and pulls the creature inside. The insect is then digested.

Dodder is a strange, total ▷ parasite. When its tiny seeds start to grow, they put up thin threads that begin to twist in ever-increasing circles. Most seedlings die, because they fail to find the right sort of plant to take their food from (the host). But if one seed finds the right host (heather or gorse for common dodder, nettles or hops for great dodder), it quickly attaches itself and pushes absorbing organs into the plant. The root of the seed then withers and dies, since the dodder plant now takes all of its food from the host.

◁ Once dodder has established itself, it produces a mass of pink threads which cover the host plant and weaken it severely. Its tiny leaves are also pink – they have no need for the green colouring (chlorophyll) that enables most plants to make food from sunlight. In late summer, dodder produces small, pink flowers, and then masses of tiny seeds.

PLANTS AND SOIL

Although there are plants almost everywhere, it is obvious that not all plants grow in all possible places. Apart from climate, one of the main factors that affects where plants grow is the soil. There are plants that seem able to grow in almost any kind of soil. Other plants, however, can be very fussy and will only grow in, say, soil with lots of chalk in it, or soil that is very acid. In this way, the kinds of plants growing in any one area can indicate the type of soil there. For example, marsh pennywort is most likely to be found in poorly drained, acid soil, so wherever you see this plant growing, you can be sure that you are on that type of soil.

Because many plants are quite specific in what they require for growth, you can use certain common species to construct a chart as shown. Here, a few species have been selected as 'indicators' of certain soil conditions. If you find any of these you can quickly read off from the chart roughly how wet or dry and how acid or alkaline the soil is.

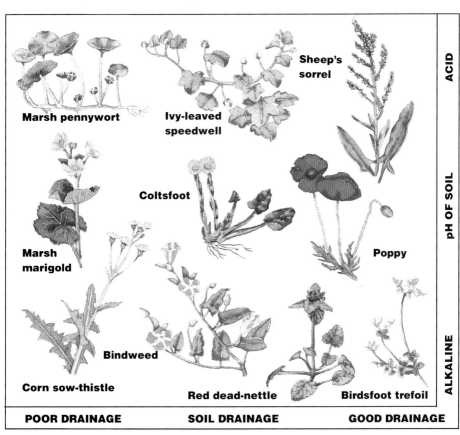

Marsh pennywort

Ivy-leaved speedwell

Sheep's sorrel

Coltsfoot

Marsh marigold

Poppy

Bindweed

Corn sow-thistle

Red dead-nettle

Birdsfoot trefoil

ACID

pH OF SOIL

ALKALINE

POOR DRAINAGE   SOIL DRAINAGE   GOOD DRAINAGE

22

If you find a reasonable area of heathland, you can be pretty certain that you are on acid soil, even though you cannot be sure whether it is sand, gravel or acidic clay. Heathers are so specific to acid soil that, if you find some growing on chalk, you can be sure that you will find a small pocket of acidic soil on top of the chalk in which they are rooted.

Underneath heathlands and some other acid soils, you may find a very distinctive soil feature known as a podsol. If you come across a quarry, road cutting or hole in the ground on heathland, have a look. Rainwater, as it passes down through the soil, picks up acids which dissolve minerals and deposit them at lower levels in the soil. Eventually, this produces a very distinctive, layered soil, sometimes with hard bands of iron in it.

PROJECT

Garden centres and some natural history suppliers sell soil-testing kits. Very accurate ones tend to be expensive, but you can buy cheap ones that give a fair idea of how acid or alkaline a sample of soil is (measured on a standard scale known as pH). If you can, buy one and test the soil from your own garden. You could then test some soil samples from other places such as heathland (which will be acid) and chalk downs (alkaline) and compare the different results.

MAN-MADE WASTELAND

Within cities, towns and industrial areas, there are a surprising number of places where flowers can thrive, and there are often uncommon species to be found. Some plants, often those with light, easily-scattered seeds, have become expert at establishing themselves quickly on bare land, even where the conditions appear to be impossible for healthy growth. For example, in some places, the waste products from factories or power stations now support a mass of orchids, whilst elsewhere, other species have found places in man-made wasteland where the conditions suit them.

Common mallow ▼
This plant, with its attractive reddish-purple flowers, is common on waste ground everywhere except in the far north.

Stinging nettle ▼
Large patches of stinging nettle are probably one of the most familiar sights on waste ground and in neglected gardens.

Red dead-nettle ▶
Very widespread throughout the region, the uppermost leaves, as well as the flowers, of this plant are often tinged with red.

Ivy-leaved toadflax ▶
The lilac flowers of ivy-leaved toadflax are a common sight on walls and waste ground throughout the summer.

◄ Common field speedwell
This plant can appear almost anywhere, wherever there is enough depth of soil for its seeds to root.

Rosebay willowherb ▼
The light, windborne seeds of this plant blow everywhere, so it is almost always one of the first species to grow on new patches of wasteland.

Oxford ragwort comes originally from Sicily, but the conditions on waste ground in Britain seem to suit it well.

◄ Dandelion
Dandelion is a familiar sight almost everywhere, even thriving in cracks in concrete or paving stones.

Greater plantain ▼
Greater plantain thrives in damp, disturbed places, such as wheel ruts and gateways.

Ground ivy ▼
A very common, highly adaptable plant that seems to be as happy on waste ground as it is in ancient woodlands.

Common chickweed ▲
If there are a reasonable amount of nutrients in the soil, chickweed will quickly establish itself and spread very rapidly.

25

FIELD AND HEDGEROW

Most of the countryside is now made up of intensively farmed land. Although large areas of this are no longer very suitable for flowers, there are still a few places where some do manage to survive. The edges of fields often have a rich mixture of plant species, whilst hedgerows and old lanes are always worth a look. Even ploughed land, if it is not sprayed with chemicals too much, can have its own selection of flowering plants, adapted to cope with the constant disturbance.

White campion ▼
Abundant in disturbed ground or open grassy areas, white campion often cross-breeds with red campion to produce hybrid plants with pink flowers.

Wild arum ▼
Also known as cuckoo-pint, the strange flower spikes of wild arum appear in spring along hedgerows and on the edges of fields.

▼ **Scarlet pimpernel**
This always looks very conspicuous in photographs, but you actually have to look quite hard to spot scarlet pimpernel in the wild.

Bindweed ▲
The pink or white flowers of bindweed are a familiar site on cultivated and disturbed ground, or along hedgerows.

▼ Cow parsley
Probably the commonest of all hedgerow and roadside plants, the white flowers of cow parsley line the edges of many roads, lanes and fields throughout the spring and early summer.

Common poppy ▼
The scarlet flowers of poppy are still familiar, although modern farming methods are slowly beginning to reduce their numbers.

Perennial sow-thistle ▼
The tall spikes and yellow flowers of this plant often stand out above the heads of the crop in which it is growing.

Goose grass ▶
By midsummer, goose grass can be found scrambling over hedges, other plants, and bare ground almost everywhere.

Sun spurge ▼
A common plant of ploughed or cultivated land, especially in gardens or along the edges of fields.

◀ Curled dock
Abundant everywhere in disturbed places, this fast-spreading and persistent weed is unpopular with farmers.

MEADOWS

Meadows are grassy areas which are mown for hay, or grazed and mown. If they are not treated with fertilisers or weedkillers, they are wonderful places to find flowers, although, sadly, many have been turned into flowerless expanses of bright-green grass. Most meadows are at their best in May or June (later in the mountains), but take care not to walk through and flatten the hay just before it is ready to cut. After hay is cut, many plants flower again, and meadows are worth revisiting in late summer.

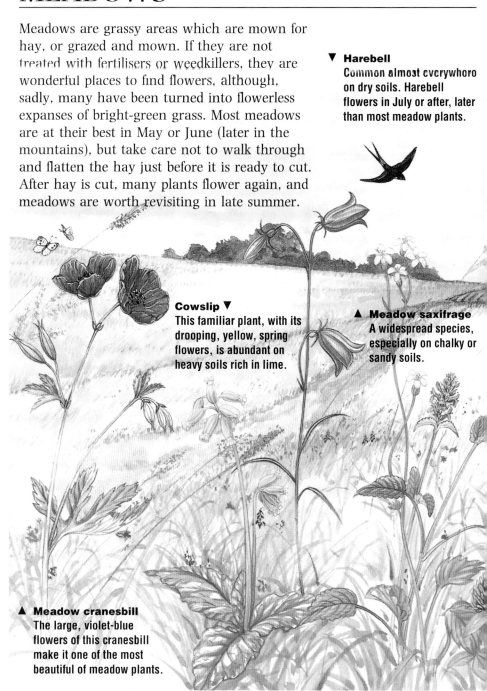

▼ Harebell
Common almost everywhere on dry soils. Harebell flowers in July or after, later than most meadow plants.

Cowslip ▼
This familiar plant, with its drooping, yellow, spring flowers, is abundant on heavy soils rich in lime.

▲ Meadow saxifrage
A widespread species, especially on chalky or sandy soils.

▲ Meadow cranesbill
The large, violet-blue flowers of this cranesbill make it one of the most beautiful of meadow plants.

PROJECT

The sheer mass of flowers in a meadow is incredible, as in this old meadow shown here. Some meadows are known to have over 40 flowers in one square metre! If you can beat 20 in a square metre, you will be doing well.

◀ Meadow buttercup
This grows in almost every meadow. Look at the flower's sepals – if they turn down, it is not meadow buttercup, but bulbous buttercup.

▲ Dyer's greenweed
Its tussocks can be seen in midsummer, especially in grazed meadows, although it is rare in the north.

◀ Betony
The wine-red flowers of betony are a distinctive feature of meadows that are cut in late summer.

◀ Red clover
A common flower of meadows, the honey-scented flowers of red clover attract many insects, especially bees.

Bugle ▶
Common both in woodlands and meadows, the purplish blue flowers of bugle attract butterflies on sunny, spring days.

PASTURE

Pastures are areas of grassland that are regularly grazed. If they are often treated with fertilisers and are bright green, they will have few wild plants, but if they have been left untouched, they make rich hunting-grounds for flowers. Good pasture grasslands can sometimes be found on old common land, chalk downs, or anywhere where the ground is too steep for farm machinery. Look out especially for small, hedged fields – these often support a wide range of flowering plants.

Common spotted orchid ▼
The tall, pink flower spikes and grey-green, spotted leaves of this plant make it easy to recognise.

Wild thyme ▼
Wild thyme forms large, low 'carpets' on any dry grassland, growing well on most types of soil.

Common rock-rose ▲
A common plant of sunny pastures with soil rich in lime, such as chalk or limestone downs.

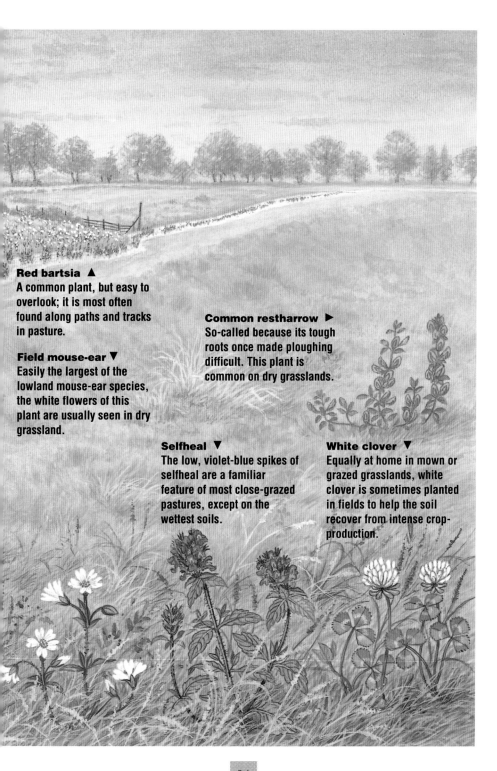

Red bartsia ▲
A common plant, but easy to overlook; it is most often found along paths and tracks in pasture.

Field mouse-ear ▼
Easily the largest of the lowland mouse-ear species, the white flowers of this plant are usually seen in dry grassland.

Common restharrow ▶
So-called because its tough roots once made ploughing difficult. This plant is common on dry grasslands.

Selfheal ▼
The low, violet-blue spikes of selfheal are a familiar feature of most close-grazed pastures, except on the wettest soils.

White clover ▼
Equally at home in mown or grazed grasslands, white clover is sometimes planted in fields to help the soil recover from intense crop-production.

WOODLAND

Woodlands can be wonderful places for flowers – and all forms of wildlife – although much depends on the type of woodland. Ancient woodlands, with plenty of sunny clearings and glades, are best, while conifer plantations are worst, with very few species. Areas of hazel or other shrubs that have recently been cut back are often especially rich in flowers. However, when the shrubs regrow, after about a year or two, and their branches start to block out the light again, everything dies back. The peak of flowering in woods is nearly always in spring and early summer.

Dog's mercury ▼
One of the commonest of old woodland plants, the unpleasant smell of dog's mercury is produced to attract the midges that pollinate it.

◄ **Greater stitchwort**
This white-flowered plant grows in large clumps in clearings and along the edges of woodland.

Herb robert ▼
A common plant of sunny clearings in woods, although it also does well in many other habitats.

Primrose ▼
A familiar spring flower, primrose is common throughout woodland, especially where there is a little extra light from above.

▲ **Enchanter's nightshade**
An inconspicuous flower of shady banks. Its fruits are covered with bristles, designed to hook onto the fur of passing animals so that its seeds will be scattered.

Coppicing is the practice of cutting shrubs back to ground level so that they sprout to produce masses of even-sized poles. This is most often done to hazel. Once, almost every wood was coppiced, but now only a few are. When out in woodland, check for areas that have been recently cleared, and see if there are numerous old stumps that have been cut back. These places are usually superb hunting grounds for both flowers and insects.

Bugle ▼
An attractive plant of woodland clearings and glades, producing masses of blue flower spires in spring.

◄ Sanicle
A plant of the shadier parts of ancient woodlands, although easily overlooked because of its inconspicuous flowers.

Common dog violet ▼
This species of violet grows almost anywhere in woods, in shade or sun. It flowers in spring, before the trees come into leaf.

Wood anemone ▼
Also known as windflower, wood anemone can occur in great drifts of white where conditions suit it.

Wood sorrel ▲
A small plant, often growing in the darker parts of woodland, usually on dry soil. Wood sorrel grows well under beech trees.

FRESH WATER

Areas of open water, whether still or flowing, almost always support a huge range of wildlife, and there are usually many different types of specially adapted flowers to be found. Not all such areas are the same – much depends on the chemicals dissolved in the water, the rate of flow, the water depth, and the soil, with different flowers for each combination of conditions. Nowadays, too, pollution plays a part, since few flowers will survive in heavily polluted waters.

Himalayan balsam ▼
Introduced into northern Europe from Asia, this attractive plant has found a home along our rivers and canals.

Yellow water-lily ▼
The large, floating leaves, yellow flowers, and bottle-shaped fruits are distinctive features of this flower.

Common water crowfoot ▼
In early summer, the surfaces of many ponds and small lakes may turn white with the flowers of this floating-leaved water plant.

Frogbit ▲
This small, floating, water plant produces special buds which sink to the bottom in autumn, then rise to the surface again in spring.

Yellow flag iris ▶
A plant of wet meadows, riversides, and pond edges, wherever soil conditions are either neutral or acidic.

Water plantain ▼
One of the commonest of the larger plants of ponds, slow-flowing rivers, canals and muddy areas.

Flowering rush ▶
The masses of pink flowers of flowering rush are a beautiful sight along the edges of rivers and lakes, especially near the coast.

White water-lily ▼
The large flowers of white water-lily, with their numerous petals and masses of yellow stamens, are unlike anything else in the water.

Amphibious bistort ▲
A strange plant that can grow both on land or in water, looking completely different in each case.

MARSH AND BOG

Marsh, bog and fen are areas of land where the soil is waterlogged for much of the year. They therefore provide a habitat in which conditions are halfway between those of open water and those of dry land. Depending on the soil and the climate, different types of wetland develop; for example, bogs are very acidic, whilst fens are more alkaline, although both are very peaty. These wetland areas are often very rich in unusual plants, and they are best visited from midsummer to early autumn for a range of species in flower.

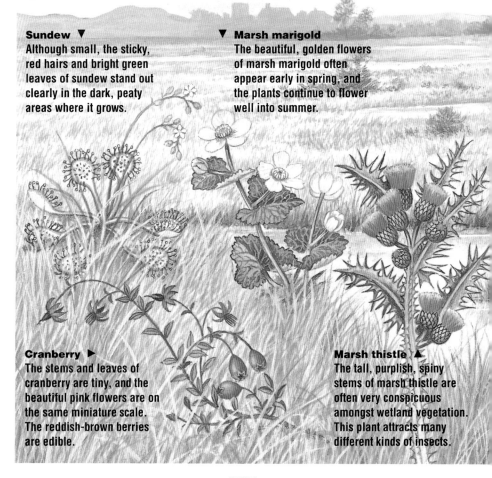

Sundew ▼
Although small, the sticky, red hairs and bright green leaves of sundew stand out clearly in the dark, peaty areas where it grows.

▼ Marsh marigold
The beautiful, golden flowers of marsh marigold often appear early in spring, and the plants continue to flower well into summer.

Cranberry ►
The stems and leaves of cranberry are tiny, and the beautiful pink flowers are on the same miniature scale. The reddish-brown berries are edible.

Marsh thistle ▲
The tall, purplish, spiny stems of marsh thistle are often very conspicuous amongst wetland vegetation. This plant attracts many different kinds of insects.

In many wetland areas, reeds are regularly cut down and their stems used for thatching and other purposes. Reed-cutting is generally good for the reed bed and the wildlife it supports. Check out the reed beds in your area and see if you can find any that have been cut recently. If you are lucky, you may come across the reed-cutters themselves, who often know a lot about local plants and animals.

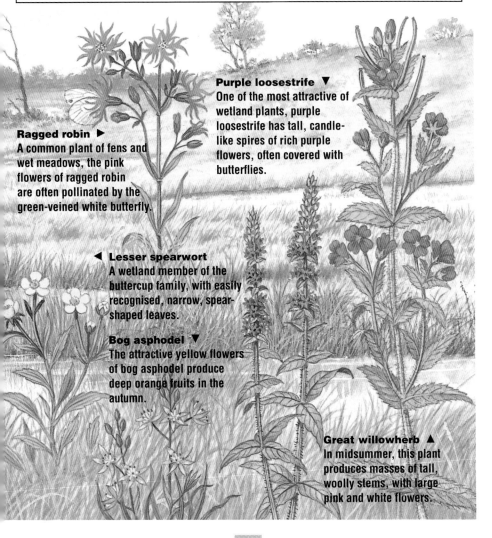

Ragged robin ▶
A common plant of fens and wet meadows, the pink flowers of ragged robin are often pollinated by the green-veined white butterfly.

Purple loosestrife ▼
One of the most attractive of wetland plants, purple loosestrife has tall, candle-like spires of rich purple flowers, often covered with butterflies.

◀ **Lesser spearwort**
A wetland member of the buttercup family, with easily recognised, narrow, spear-shaped leaves.

Bog asphodel ▼
The attractive yellow flowers of bog asphodel produce deep orange fruits in the autumn.

Great willowherb ▲
In midsummer, this plant produces masses of tall, woolly stems, with large pink and white flowers.

HEATHLAND

Heathlands are wide, open places where heather, ling and/or gorse are the main plants. Heaths may be open over their whole area, or there may be parts where birch, juniper, pine or other trees invade them. In fact, heaths are not natural; they were created by the clearance of natural forest by early farmers. The presence of soil high in acidity caused the cleared land to develop into heathland. For flowers, heaths are at their best in late summer when all the heathers are in flower, attracting swarms of many different insects.

▼ Gorse
Bushes of gorse are a common sight on most heaths, where their yellow flowers brighten up the scenery in spring.

Tormentil ▼
This tiny trailing plant is easily overlooked, but it is common all over the grassier parts of heaths.

Bell heather ▲
With ling, this is the commonest heathland plant. In late summer, its masses of flowers can turn dry areas of heath a beautiful deep red.

Ling ▲
Often the dominant plant of heathland, in both dry and damp areas. Its flowers are smaller and paler in colour than those of bell heather.

Wood sage ▼
Look for this flower around bushes and along the edges of heathland. Its crinkly leaves have a strong scent.

Chickweed wintergreen ▼
This attractive little flower is a plant of northern moorlands and open woods. It is rare on the warmer heaths further south.

Cross-leaved heath ▼
This distinctive, grey-leaved plant, with a bushy top of pink flowers, grows only on the wetter parts of heaths.

◀ **Heath speedwell**
This flower forms one of the few splashes of blue colour in the heathland scene, flowering from May onwards.

MOUNTAINOUS UPLAND

As you go higher up a mountain, there are less and less trees, and the ones that do grow begin to get smaller and more stunted. Eventually, you reach a point where there are no longer any trees at all, and the vegetation is naturally open. You are then above the tree line. This open land above the tree line is often rich in specialised mountain plants. Many of them have tight 'cushions' of leaves, and their flowers are often brilliantly coloured to attract the few insects that are able to survive so high up.

Bilberry ▼
Bilberry can be found at many different heights on a mountain slope, as long as the soil is acid.

Purple saxifrage ▼
This plant produces masses of purple flowers on tiny leaf 'cushions' as soon as the snow has melted.

Kidney vetch ▼
Although also common in the lowlands, kidney vetch does well in mountain areas with soil rich in lime.

Yellow mountain saxifrage ▶
This lovely flower is found only near streams and wet rocks in high mountain areas or in the far north.

▲ Alpine lady's mantle
An attractive, low-growing plant with silvery leaves and greenish flowers. It is found in mountain pastures.

40

Some mountains have very few interesting flowers on them, however hard you search. Without doubt, limestone mountain areas are best, or mountains with lime-rich, mica schist rocks. These rocks are worn down by wind and rain (eroded) quite quickly, so there is a constant supply of lime in the soil which suits many plant species. Check maps that tell you the kinds of rocks there are in an area, or consult local guide books to find out where limestone mountains can be found.

◄ Common eyebright
Not really a mountain specialist, but frequently found high up on mountain grasslands.

Mountain pansy ▼
The beautiful, yellow or purple flowers of mountain pansies are larger and more colourful than those of lowland pansies.

Autumn felwort ►
Widespread in the lowlands, but also frequent in mountain pastures with plenty of lime in the soil.

Snow gentian ►
Unusually for a high mountain plant, snow gentian is an annual – it grows from seed, flowers, produces seeds and dies, all in one short, mountain-top summer.

THE COASTLINE

The coast is a superb place for flowers. Unspoilt coasts are made up of many different habitats, each with different species of flowering plant. These include rocky cliffs, sand dunes, saltmarshes, shingle and coastal grasslands. In addition, other kinds of habitats near the coast will be influenced by the mild climate, with perhaps a hint of salt in the air, and many plants do very well under these conditions. This makes any flower-hunting visit to the coast in summertime very rewarding.

Sea holly ▼
A common plant of sand dunes, both the bright blue flowers and the thick, blue grey leaves of sea holly bear sharp spines.

Sea sandwort ▼
Sea sandwort often grows in masses, around or above the high tidemark, on sandy and shingly coasts.

Prickly saltwort ▲
Prickly saltwort seems to survive in the most extraordinary places, even where it is regularly washed over by the sea.

Sea rocket ▼
Sea rocket has the typical, fleshy grey leaves of many coastal plants, designed to save water in the salty environment.

◄ **Common scurvy-grass**
So-called because the fleshy, edible leaves were once eaten by sailors to prevent 'scurvy', a disease caused by lack of vitamin C.

Thrift ▼
When thrift flowers in May or June, it is one of the most impressive natural sights, turning huge areas of clifftop and saltmarsh a beautiful rose pink.

Shingle looks like the most inhospitable of habitats, with no soil, constantly moving stones, and regular drenchings from the sea. Yet some plants, like this sea kale, not only survive, but do well.

▲ Common storksbill
A low-growing plant with pink flowers, most often found in bare, sandy areas or open grassland.

◄ Yellow horned poppy
One of the most striking of coastal plants, with its big yellow flowers, and long, grey-green seed pods.

Sea campion ►
Found in big clumps on cliffs and shingle, sea campion produces masses of white flowers in early summer, almost hiding the leaves.

MISTLETOE AND DOCKS

MISTLETOE
Viscum album
Familiar plant, widely used as a decoration at Christmas. Occurs as a partial parasite on apple, poplar and other trees. Fl 2-4; P.

GENERAL FEATURES

All of the plants shown here have small, insignificant flowers, although otherwise they have little in common. Mistletoe lives by taking some of the nutrients it needs from trees and has no contact with the ground. The other species are more normal in their way of life, although stinging nettle has unusually strong defences – its painful stings.

HABITATS

Mistletoe lives on just a few types of tree, and is commonest in warm areas where the soil is rich in lime. Docks, fat hen and stinging nettle all live in disturbed areas, especially cultivated land. Amphibious bistort can grow on land or in water, looking quite different in each case.

After Christmas, try seeding mistletoe onto your apple tree by making a nick in the bark of a branch, and rubbing a berry into it. Alternatively, put the berries out for the birds, and let them do the work! The mistletoe will have little harmful effect on your tree.

STINGING NETTLE ▷
Urtica dioica
H 30–60cm. Familiar, upright plant, with stinging hairs all over. Male flowers in long green spikes, females shorter. Fl 6-9; F, W; P.

AMPHIBIOUS BISTORT
Polygonum amphibium
In water, produces oval leaves, and dense, pink flower heads; on land, it has erect stems to 30cm, narrower leaves, and thinner flower heads. Fl 6-8; M, R; P.

FAT HEN ▲
Chenopodium album
H 30-100cm. Common weed, with leaves and stems covered in greyish-white, mealy substance. Leaves roughly diamond-shaped, toothed. Flowers small and greenish. Fl 7-10; F, W; A.

COMMON SORREL
Rumex acetosa
H 30-80cm. Like a small dock, but with arrow-shaped leaves at base. Reddish flowers, in thin, branched spikes; male and female plants separate. Fl 5-6; F, W, Pa; P.

CURLED DOCK ▷
Rumex crispus
H 30-100cm. Strong-growing, tall plant. Leaves narrow, usually rounded at base, with crinkled edges. Flowers reddish, on long spikes. Fl 6-10; C, F, Wa; P.

STITCHWORTS AND OTHERS

GREATER STITCHWORT
Stellaria holostea
H 20-60cm. A sprawling
plant, often in large clumps.
Leaves narrow, greyish, with
finely toothed edges.
Flowers white with five
petals, divided halfway.
Fl 5-7; Wd, Md; P.

GENERAL FEATURES

Apart from saltwort, all the plants shown here
are members of the pink family. They usually
have a whorl of five petals (although often each
is divided into two) and opposite leaves in pairs.
The stitchworts and chickweeds all have white
flowers. Saltwort has spiny leaves.

HABITATS

The stitchworts are usually perennial plants
(plants which live on from year to year), so they
tend to grow in undisturbed places like
hedgerows, woodland edges and meadows.
Chickweed is an annual weed (a plant that
grows from seed, flowers, forms seeds and dies
all in one year), so it prefers disturbed ground.
Saltwort and sea sandwort both grow on sandy
or muddy seashores.

If you look closely at a stem
of chickweed, you'll find a
curious feature – a single,
thin line of hairs, which
changes side at each node.
The purpose of these hairs is
not known for certain. It may
be that they help to channel
water down the stem from
one pair of leaves to the
next. At each leaf node,
some of the water is
absorbed and kept in reserve
in case of drought.

SALTWORT ▲
Salsola kali
H 20-40cm. A distinctive
sprawling or creeping plant,
with fleshy, prickle-tipped
leaves and small, greenish,
five-petalled flowers.
Fl 7–10; C; A.

SEA SANDWORT ▲
Honkenya peploides
H to 20cm. A spreading
plant, with short, erect, leafy
stems, often in large
patches. Leaves fleshy,
bright green. Flowers small,
greenish-white. Fl 5-8; C; P.

COMMON CHICKWEED ▼
Stellaria media
H to 30cm. Sprawling, fast-
growing plant. Leaves heart-
shaped, stalked. Flowers
white, with deeply cut petals.
Very common. Fl all year.
F, W; A.

FIELD MOUSE-EAR ▲
Cerastium arvense
H to 30cm. Sprawling plant
like greater stitchwort, but
very hairy all over. Flowers
in loose clusters, with petals
twice as long as sepals.
Fl 5-7; Md, Pa; P.

**LESSER
STITCHWORT** ▲
Stellaria graminea
H 20-50cm. Similar to
greater stitchwort, but leaves
smooth-edged, not so grey.
Flowers smaller, with petals
divided more than halfway.
Fl 6-9; Md, Pa; P.

CAMPIONS AND RELATIVES

GENERAL FEATURES

Campions, catchflies and pinks are closely related to stitchworts, with similar, although larger, flowers (up to 4cm across). In bladder campion, the calyx (group of sepals) is distinctly swollen, and very noticeable. In all these species, the leaves are in opposite pairs.

a   b

HABITATS

Campions and pinks have spread into virtually all habitats. White campion and bladder campion are commonest in disturbed areas, red campion is common almost everywhere, and sea campion has adapted to life on the coast. Maiden pink is most likely to be found in undisturbed grassland areas, whilst ragged robin thrives in marshes and fens.

Campions have separate male and female plants. Even after flowering you can tell the difference by counting the lines on the calyx – there are 20 lines on females (a), 10 on males (b).

WHITE CAMPION
Silene latifolia var alba
H 30-100cm. An upright plant, with large, white flowers with petals notched to about halfway. Leaves oval, covered with sticky hairs. Fl 5-9; F, W; A or P.

BLADDER CAMPION
Silene vulgaris
H 25-90cm. Upright, branching plant, usually hairless, with greyish leaves. Flowers white, about 2cm across, with stamens protruding distinctly. Fl 5-9; Md, Pa, F; P.

SEA CAMPION
Silene maritima
H 10-25cm. A spreading low plant, usually hairless, forming mats. Leaves small, greyish, paired. Flowers white, with stamens less protruding than bladder campion. Fl 5-8; C, Mt; P.

RAGGED ROBIN
Lychnis flos cuculi
H 35-70cm. Spreading plant with erect, flowering shoots. Lower leaves spoon-shaped, upper ones narrow. Flowers large, pink, with 'ragged' petals. Fl 5-8; M, Md; P.

RED CAMPION
Silene dioica
H 30-90cm. Upright, soft-haired plant, numerous flowers rose-pink. Male and female flowers on separate plants. Fl 5-10; C, F, Wd, Md, Pa; B or P.

MAIDEN PINK
Dianthus deltoides
H 15-45cm. Tufted, hairless plant. Flowers pink, 1-2cm across, with fringed petals marked with dots and lines. Fl 6-9; Md, Pa; P.

WATER-LILIES AND OTHERS

GENERAL FEATURES

The water-lilies are large, aquatic plants, rooted in mud but with floating, kidney-shaped leaves. White water-lily flowers are up to 10cm across, produced at water level, while yellow water-lily flowers are smaller, and produced on stalks above the water. Their fruits, when ripe, look like old-fashioned brandy bottles.

HABITATS

White water-lilies grow in lakes and ponds, where the water may be acid or alkaline, but not fast-flowing. Yellow water-lilies are found in similar places, but are also frequent in rivers, unless they are polluted. Marsh marigolds and globe flowers are plants of damp grassland and woodland, whilst stinking hellebore is a woodland plant.

White water-lilies are one of a group of plants whose flowers close up for the night. As evening approaches, the petals gradually curl inwards, sometimes trapping insects inside. This conserves heat, and reduces the risk of damage from, for example, strong winds or heavy rain.

WHITE WATER-LILY
Nymphaea alba
Grows in water up to 3m deep. Leaves thick and leathery, oval with a deep cleft. Flowers white, with about 20 petals, and yellow stamens. Fl 6-9; R; P.

YELLOW WATER-LILY
Nuphar lutea
Aquatic, growing in water up to 5m deep. Leaves similar to white water-lily. Flowers 2–3cm across, yellow, on long stalks above water level. Fl 6-9; R; P.

MARSH MARIGOLD
Caltha palustris
H 10-40cm. A clump-forming plant, with heart-shaped leaves. Flowers yellow, with five sepals but no petals. Fl 4-8; M, Mt, Pa; P.

STINKING HELLEBORE
Helleborus foetidus
H 20-80cm. Robust, bushy plant with unpleasant smell. Leaves deeply divided, flowers green with red edges. Poisonous. Fl 2-4; Wd; P.

PROJECT

Aquaria are usually used to house fish and aquatic animals, but you could use one simply to keep a selection of interesting aquatic plants, which you will be able to observe throughout the year. Use an ordinary aquarium, and choose small aquatics such as frogbit, Canadian pondweed, or duckweed. The addition of a few pond animals will help to keep conditions in the aquarium healthy and stable. Make sure you put the aquarium in good light.

GLOBEFLOWER
Trollius europaeus
H 20-70cm. An upright plant. Leaves with 3-5 deep lobes, hairless. Flowers yellow with up to 15 petal-like sepals. Fl 5-8; Md, Pa, Wd; P.

THE BUTTERCUP FAMILY 1

WOOD ANEMONE
Anemone nemorosa
H 10-30cm. A spreading
plant with leafy, flowering
stems, forming large
patches. Leaves deeply
divided and toothed. Flowers
white, often pinkish below.
Fl 3-5; Wd, Md; P.

GENERAL FEATURES

Despite their differences in appearance, all the
flowers shown here belong to the buttercup
family. A common feature of this family is the
variable number of petals and sepals, and the
large number of stamens in the centre of the
flower. The petals of columbine flowers have a
hollow, nectar-secreting spur at their base.
Meadow-rue and traveller's joy have flowers
that seem to be all stamens.

HABITATS

Wood anemone and hepatica are normally
woodland plants (hepatica is common
throughout Europe, but not native in Britain).
The others are mainly plants of open places,
although columbine can happily survive in
shade or full sun.

Buttercup remedies
Many members of the
buttercup family were once
used as medicines, and
some still are. Although
these plants are often
poisonous, in small
controlled quantities their
juices can be used
medicinally. Both columbine
and lesser celandine, for
example, were once used to
treat scurvy (a disease
caused by lack of vitamin C).
The fresh, washed leaves of
another species, hepatica,
were crushed to a pulp, then
applied to cuts and grazes to
help them heal quickly.

Are these flowers wind-pollinated or insect-pollinated? Try putting muslin bags over some buds of any of these flowers to keep out the insects. If any of them develop fruit, they will have been wind-pollinated – the flowers relying on insects to transfer their pollen will not produce seed.

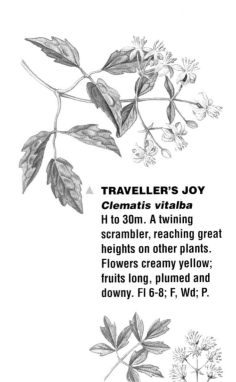

TRAVELLER'S JOY
Clematis vitalba
H to 30m. A twining scrambler, reaching great heights on other plants. Flowers creamy yellow; fruits long, plumed and downy. Fl 6-8; F, Wd; P.

MEADOW-RUE ▶
Thalictrum flavum
H 50-100cm. An upright, usually unbranched plant with masses of yellow flowers, consisting mainly of stamens. Fl 6-8; M, Pa; P.

HEPATICA ▼
Hepatica nobilis
H 5-20cm. Low, tufted plant. Leaves 3-lobed, all growing from base. Flowers with 6-10 segments, blue, purple or white. Fl 3-4; Wd; P.

COLUMBINE ▲
Aquilegia vulgaris
H 30-100cm. An upright, often branched plant, with 3-lobed leaves. Flowers blue, violet or white, with long spurs. Fl 5-7; Wd, Md, Pa; P.

THE BUTTERCUP FAMILY 2

GENERAL FEATURES

All the flowers shown here belong to the scientific genus *Ranunculus*, part of the large buttercup family, although they do not all have the English name 'buttercup'. These plants have simple flowers with several petals, an outer ring of sepals, and numerous stamens. Most buttercups have yellow flowers, although the water-crowfoots all have white flowers.

HABITATS

All these buttercups grow in grassland, each growing best in slightly different conditions. Bulbous buttercup is generally found in the driest places, lesser spearwort thrives in wet places, while the water-crowfoots grow in water, or on wet mud. Celandine is common in woods.

Creeping buttercup

Bulbous buttercup

Lesser Celandine

There are several similar-looking yellow buttercups, but these can be easily told apart by examining the flower, the flower stalk and the leaves.

MEADOW BUTTERCUP
Ranunculus acris
H 20-90cm. Upright plant, with leaves divided into 3-7 fan-like segments – top leaflet has no stalk. Flowers yellow, with smooth stalks; sepals not turned back down stem, as in some other species. Fl 4-8; Md, Pa; P.

BULBOUS BUTTERCUP

BULBOUS BUTTERCUP
Ranunculus bulbosus
H 15-45cm. Similar to
meadow buttercup, but
smaller, with flowers on
furrowed stalks, and sepals
strongly bent back down
stem. Fl 4–7; Md, Pa; P.

CREEPING BUTTERCUP
Ranunculus repens
H 15-60cm. A creeping plant,
with long, leafy runners.
Flowers on furrowed stalks,
sepals not bent back. Fl 5-9;
F, Md, Pa; P.

LESSER SPEARWORT
Ranunculus flammula
H 10-60cm. An upright or
creeping plant. Flowers like
buttercups, but stems hollow,
and leaves undivided. Fl 5-8;
M, Md, Pa; P.

LESSER CELANDINE
Ranunculus ficaria
H 5-25cm. Low, bulbous
plant, with rosette of heart-
shaped leaves at the base of
stem. Flowers with up to 12
narrow petals. Fl 3-5; Wd; P.

WATER-CROWFOOT
Ranunculus aquatilis
Aquatic plant, with floating
lobed leaves, and finely-
divided leaves underwater.
Flowers white, 1.5-2cm
across. Fl 5-8; R; P.

POPPIES AND OTHERS

COMMON POPPY
Papaver rhoeas
H 20-60cm. An upright plant, with rough-haired stems and leaves. Leaves deeply lobed and toothed. Flowers scarlet, with black blotches at base of petals. Fl 6-9; F, W; A.

GENERAL FEATURES

The poppies are a distinctive and well-known group. They have two large sepals enclosing the bud which fall off when the flower opens. The flowers have four petals, usually red or orange, and a mass of stamens. The fruit develops into a capsule, and the shape of this helps to tell similar species apart. The yellow horned poppy is similar, but has yellow flowers. Horse-radish and garlic mustard are both members of the mustard family.

HABITATS

Poppies are annual plants, needing disturbed soil to survive. They therefore grow best in ploughed fields, waste ground and new road-cuttings. Yellow horned poppy is a specialist plant of shingle beaches, where little else survives.

The different species of poppy all look very similar. A good way of identifying one from another is by taking a close look at the seed capsules.

Common poppy Long-headed poppy

Bristly poppy Pale poppy

GARLIC MUSTARD ▼
Alliaria petiolata
H 30-100cm. Upright plant, leaves yellowish-green, smelling of garlic when crushed. Fl 4-5; F, Wd; B.

HORSE-RADISH
Armoracia rusticana
H 40-100cm. Stout, upright plant, with large, oval leaves up to 50cm long. Flowers small, white, in much-branched inflorescence.
Fl 5-6; F, W; P.

FUMITORY ▲
Fumaria officinalis
H 10-50cm. A scrambling plant, with greyish-green leaves, divided into segments. Flowers pinkish-purple, producing round fruit.
Fl 5-10; F, W; A.

PROJECT

Poppy capsules are like special seed dispensers, letting out small amounts of seed at a time. Find some poppies with ripe capsules and watch them to see how far the wind has to bend each stem to release the seeds. If the air is too still, try moving a stem to see how many seeds come out at each position.

YELLOW HORNED ▼
POPPY
Glaucium flavum
H 25-35cm. An upright plant with large flowers. Seed capsules can be 30cm long.
Fl 6-9; C; B or P.

THE MUSTARD FAMILY

GENERAL FEATURES

The plants of the mustard family are usually quite easily recognised, because they all have a similar flower structure. Each flower has four petals, arranged roughly in a cross, and each petal has a main lobe, with a claw at right angles to it. They may be many different colours. These plants also often have distinctive, long, narrow fruits.

HABITATS

Members of this family can be found everywhere, from seashores to high mountains. Cuckoo flower is a plant of damp meadows, while scurvy grass and sea-rocket are most likely to be found on the coast. Hairy bitter-cress, shepherd's-purse and black mustard are most common in disturbed ground.

Cuckoo flower, and many related crucifers, are important food plants for several butterflies in the caterpillar stage, especially orange-tips and green-veined whites. The adults also visit the flowers to feast on the nectar.

CUCKOO FLOWER
Cardamine pratensis
H 15-60cm. An erect plant with pale, lilac-pink flowers, 1.5-2cm across. The narrow fruits are up to 4cm long.
Fl 4-6; M, Md, Pa; P.

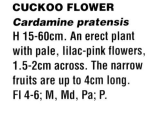

SHEPHERD'S-PURSE
Capsella bursa-pastoris
H 6-40cm. Upright plant, with rosette of lobed leaves at base of stem. Fruits heart-shaped, with a bristle point in the notch. Fl all year; F, W; A or B.

HAIRY BITTER-CRESS
Cardamine hirsuta
H 6-30cm. Small, upright plant, with rosette of leaves at base of stem and tiny, white flowers. Fl 2-11; F, W; A.

BLACK MUSTARD
Brassica nigra
H 30-100cm. An upright plant, bristly near the base, almost hairless higher up. Flowers yellow on short stalks, in a long spike. Fl 5-8; C, W; A.

SEA ROCKET
Cakile maritima
H 10-45cm. A spreading or upright, hairless, greyish plant. Leaves fleshy, varying from lobed to unlobed. Flowers pink or white, fruit egg-shaped. Fl 6-9; C; A.

COMMON SCURVY-GRASS
Cochlearia officinalis
H 5-40cm. A spreading or upright, fleshy, hairless plant. White flowers produce globe-shaped fruit. Fl 4-8; C, Mt; B or P.

STONECROPS AND SUNDEWS

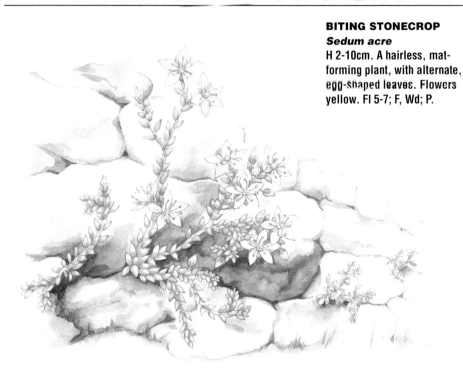

BITING STONECROP
Sedum acre
H 2-10cm. A hairless, mat-
forming plant, with alternate,
egg-shaped leaves. Flowers
yellow. Fl 5-7; F, Wd; P.

GENERAL FEATURES

The stonecrops have small, fleshy leaves, and starry, five-pointed flowers which are usually white or yellow. Sundews are easily recognised by their leaves, which are covered with red, sticky, curled, insect-catching hairs. There are three species in northern Europe, each with differently shaped leaves.

HABITATS

The stonecrops, as their name suggests, grow on rocks and cliffs, or occasionally on shingle. They are commonest near the coast or in mountain areas, although some can be found on the walls and roofs of built-up areas. Sundews thrive in wet, boggy areas while weld grows in dry, lime-rich, grassy places, such as old quarries.

Common sundew

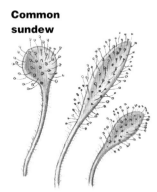

Great sundew   **Long-leaved sundew**

There are three different types of sundew to be found; you can tell them apart by the shapes and sizes of their leaves.

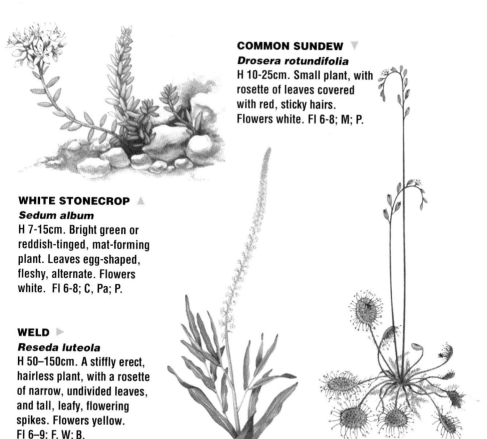

COMMON SUNDEW ▽
Drosera rotundifolia
H 10-25cm. Small plant, with
rosette of leaves covered
with red, sticky hairs.
Flowers white. Fl 6-8; M; P.

WHITE STONECROP ◭
Sedum album
H 7-15cm. Bright green or
reddish-tinged, mat-forming
plant. Leaves egg-shaped,
fleshy, alternate. Flowers
white. Fl 6-8; C, Pa; P.

WELD ▷
Reseda luteola
H 50–150cm. A stiffly erect,
hairless plant, with a rosette
of narrow, undivided leaves,
and tall, leafy, flowering
spikes. Flowers yellow.
Fl 6–9; F, W; B.

HOW TO FIND

Sundews are plants of acid, boggy
places. They are reasonably
common, but not easy to find.
First, look for wet places marked as
bogs or marshes on maps; those
surrounded by heathland are best,
as they are most acidic and least
polluted. When looking, remember
that sundews are small so you
have to look hard. For great
sundew (shown here), look in the
really wet parts of bogs; for
common sundew and long-leaved
sundew, look in slightly drier parts.

SAXIFRAGES

GENERAL FEATURES

The saxifrages are mainly plants of mountain areas, although they are often grown in gardens for their masses of beautiful flowers on tiny mats of foliage. Lowland species, such as meadow saxifrage, tend to be taller, without the tight cushion of leaves. Meadowsweet is actually a member of the rose family (see pp.64–67), close relatives of the saxifrages.

HABITATS

Yellow mountain saxifrage is most commonly found in wet places in mountain areas. Meadow saxifrage was once very common, growing in meadows with well-drained, low-acid soils, but it has suffered from the loss of its habitat to developers and farmers. Purple saxifrage does best on limestone rocks in mountains.

There are actually two widespread species of golden saxifrage. Golden saxifrage has leaves arranged in opposite pairs, whilst alternate-leaved golden saxifrage (above), has rounded, kidney-shaped leaves arranged alternately.

YELLOW MOUNTAIN SAXIFRAGE
Saxifraga aizoides
H 5–20cm. Spreading plant with upright, flowering stems. Leaves small and narrow. Yellow or orange flowers, petals sometimes spotted. Fl 6–9; Mt, M; P.

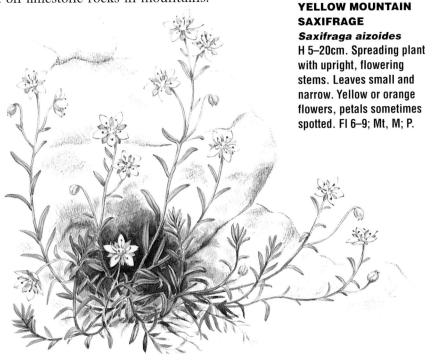

GOLDEN SAXIFRAGE
Chrysosplenium oppositifolium
H 5–15cm. A very low, patch-forming plant, with many creeping, leafy stems. Stems square and hairy. Yellow flowers have four sepals but no petals. Fl 4–6; M, Wd; P.

MEADOWSWEET
Filipendula ulmaria
H 60–120cm. Upright plant with divided leaves on red stalks. Creamy, fragrant flowers, massed together at the tops of the many stems. Fl 6–9; M, Md, Pa; P.

PURPLE SAXIFRAGE
Saxifraga oppositifolia
H up to 6cm. Very low, mat-forming plant, with single, purple flowers on stems growing directly from the mat. Fl 3–8; Mt; P.

PROJECT

A few mountain flowers, such as purple saxifrage or snowbell, actually begin to flower before the winter snow has melted from over them. Their flowers push up through the snow into the light, before the rest of the plant is visible. Look out for this next time you are in the mountains, and carefully measure the depth of snow that the flower has grown through.

MEADOW SAXIFRAGE
Saxifraga granulata
H 10–50cm, Erect, hairy plant which produces little bulbs below the base of its lower leaves. Flowers white, in branched clusters. Fl 5–6; Md, Pa; P.

ROSES AND THEIR RELATIVES 1

DOG ROSE
Rosa canina
H up to 3m. Small shrub with arching stems bearing hooked prickles. Leaves with 2–3 pairs of leaflets. Flowers pink, rarely white, 4–5cm across. Fl 6–7; F, Wd; P.

GENERAL FEATURES

The rose family is one of the largest plant families in Europe. It is a very variable group, but most of its members have regular, five-petalled flowers, with masses of stamens in the middle, and petals separated from each other. The petals and sepals are attached to the rim of a distinct cup which surrounds the centre of the flower. The leaves are always alternate (not opposite), and have an extra, leaf-like lobe at the base of their stalks known as a stipule. Many members of the family are shrubs or small trees, and they frequently bear fleshy, edible fruit, such as blackberries, strawberries, or sloes. As one species or another, they can occur in virtually every habitat.

Many of our cultivated fruits have actually been developed from the rose family. Strawberries, plums, raspberries, blackberries, peaches, and many others are in this family. In fact, many are native to north Europe, and the wild forms are often equally tasty, especially raspberries and blackberries.

WILD BLACKBERRY
Rubus fruticosus
H 1–3m. A scrambling shrub, with arching, prickly stems. Leaves with 3–5 leaflets. Flowers pink or white, black fruit edible, very variable in taste and shape. Abundant. Fl 5–9; F, W, Wd; P.

WILD RASPBERRY
Rubus idaeus
H 0.5–2m. More upright than blackberry, with slenderer prickles. Leaves with 3–7 leaflets. Flowers small, white, fruit red when ripe, edible. Fl 5–8; Wd; P.

GREAT BURNET
Sanguisorba officinalis
H 0.5–1m. Erect herb, with leaves divided into toothed leaflets. Red, oblong flower heads. Fl 6–9; Md, Pa; P.

SALAD BURNET
Sanguisorba minor
H 15–40cm. Herb, with rosette of leaves at base of stem. Edible as salad, tastes rather like cucumber. Fl 5–8; Md, Pa; P.

AGRIMONY
Agrimonia eupatoria
H 30–60cm. Upright herb, with leaves divided into numerous small and large leaflets. Flowers yellow, in spikes; fruits with hooked hairs. Fl 6–8; F, Md, Pa; P.

ROSES AND THEIR RELATIVES 2

WILD STRAWBERRY
Fragaria vesca
H 5–30cm. Herb, with long
runners. Leaves divided into
three leaflets. Flowers white,
petals longer than sepals.
Fruit red when ripe, edible.
Fl 4–7; Wd, F; P.

GENERAL FEATURES

These herbaceous, or non-woody, members of
the rose family share the same general
characteristics as the plants on pp.64–65.
Amongst these, only the wild strawberry has a
fleshy, edible fruit. The fruits of wood avens are
covered with hooks, designed to catch onto the
fur or feathers of animals and birds to help
spread the seeds.

HABITATS

Wild strawberry grows in dry, usually sunny,
locations, from railway banks to chalky downs.
Silverweed is common on disturbed ground,
whilst tormentil needs more stable situations,
almost always on acid soil. Wood avens grows
in shady places, especially woods.

Barren strawberry looks very
similar to wild strawberry,
but – as the name suggests –
it does not produce edible
fruit. The flowers differ in
that the petals are shorter
than the sepals, and there
are clear gaps between each
petal. The leaves are a
similar shape, but duller,
bluish-green in colour.

SILVERWEED ▲
Potentilla anserina
H to 10cm only. A creeping
herb, with long, thin, reddish
runners, and silvery leaves
in rosettes. Flowers yellow,
up to 2cm across. Fl 5–9; F,
Md; P.

PROJECT

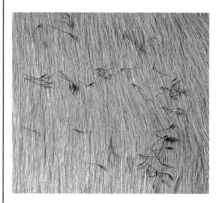

Whenever you take your dog for a walk
in late summer or autumn, check its
coat over afterwards for fruit and seeds.
It is surprising what a dog will pick up
in the countryside, and shows just how
effective such seed-scattering methods
are. If you cannot identify the seeds, try
planting them to see what comes up,
and keep a list of the species you find.

◁ **TORMENTIL**
Potentilla erecta
H up to 20cm, but often very
short. Scrambling or
creeping herb, with branched
stems and no runners.
Flowers yellow, with four
petals. Fl 5–8; H, Pa; P.

WOOD AVENS ▷
Geum urbanum
H 30–60cm. Upright herb,
with rosette of leaves, each
divided into unequal-
sized pairs of leaflets.
Flowers yellow, 1–1.5cm
across, with sepals longer
than petals. Fl 5–9; Wd; P.

THE PEA FAMILY 1

TUFTED VETCH
Vicia cracca
H up to 2m. A scrambling,
downy herb. Leaves divided
into pairs of silvery-
haired, narrow leaflets,
ending in tendrils. Flowers
purplish-blue. Fl 6–8; Md, W,
M; P.

GENERAL FEATURES

The pea family is an enormous family, with many thousands of species worldwide, yet its members are easily recognised by their distinctive flowers. These are all of the same structure, just like sweet pea flowers, although often on a much smaller scale. The flowers are irregular in shape, with a large standard petal at the back, two wing petals at the sides, and two lower petals forming a boat-shaped 'keel'. Many of the vetches and wild peas are scrambling plants, making use of their long tendrils, although this is not a characteristic of the whole family. Gorse and spiny restharrow both have spines. These plants grow in a wide range of different habitats.

Most vetches and peas have tendrils. These are special, coiling, hair-like structures, usually coming out of the leaves, that attach the vetch to other plants and support it. Tendrils can be branched or simple. Some are long and coil several times around another stem, while others grip more lightly.

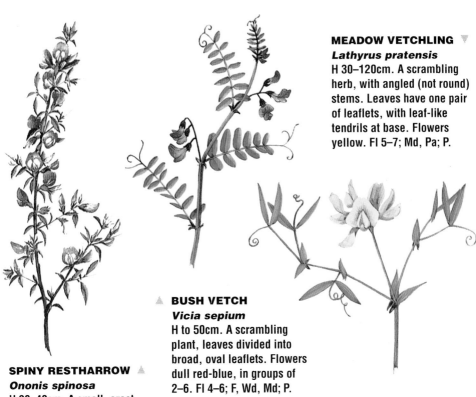

MEADOW VETCHLING

Lathyrus pratensis
H 30–120cm. A scrambling herb, with angled (not round) stems. Leaves have one pair of leaflets, with leaf-like tendrils at base. Flowers yellow. Fl 5–7; Md, Pa; P.

BUSH VETCH

Vicia sepium
H to 50cm. A scrambling plant, leaves divided into broad, oval leaflets. Flowers dull red-blue, in groups of 2–6. Fl 4–6; F, Wd, Md; P.

SPINY RESTHARROW

Ononis spinosa
H 20–40cm. A small, erect shrubby plant, with pale spines on stem. Flowers deep pinkish-purple, with wings shorter than keel. Fl 5–9; Pa; P.

COMMON GORSE

Ulex europaeus
H 1–2.5m. Spiny evergreen shrub. Spines straight, furrowed, to 2.5cm long; virtually no leaves. Flowers yellow, smelling of coconut. Flowers all year round, mainly spring. H, C, Pa; P.

COMMON REST-HARROW

Ononis repens
H to 40cm. A creeping or partly-erect herb, usually without spines, but sticky-haired. Flowers purplish-pink, with wings equal to keel. Fl 6–9; Pa, Md, C; P.

THE PEA FAMILY 2

GENERAL FEATURES

All the flowers on this page are also members of the pea family, and have the same general characteristics as those on pp.68–69. However, the flowers are often individually small, grouped together in heads, so their structure is harder to see. A particular feature of the clovers is their three-lobed (trifoliate) leaves. The lucky 'four-leaved clover' is an abnormal rarity.

HABITATS

Clovers are generally plants of grassland, grazed or ungrazed. They are commonest near the coast, and on chalky or clay soils. Kidney vetch is not a clover, but shares some of their features; it is commonest on chalk and limestone downs, or in coastal areas with soil rich in lime.

The flowers of clover are very rich in nectar as a means of attracting insects. If you carefully pull off individual flowers, and suck the base of the white tube, you will get a lovely taste of fresh honey (unless an insect has just visited).

RED CLOVER
Trifolium pratense
H 10–40cm. A hairy, erect herb. Leaves 3-lobed, each leaflet marked with white crescent. Flowers reddish. Fl 5–9; Md, Pa; P.

WHITE CLOVER
Trifolium repens
H 10-50cm. Creeping herb, with long-stalked, 3-lobed leaves, usually with white-spotted leaflets. Flowers white, in small, round heads. Fl 6–9; Md, Pa; P.

HOP TREFOIL
Trifolium campestre
H 10–30cm. An upright herb, with 3-lobed leaves. Flowers small, yellow, with 20–30 grouped together into globe-shaped heads. Brown fruits look like tiny hops. Fl 6–9; Md, Pa, F; A.

BIRDSFOOT TREFOIL
Lotus corniculatus
H 10–40cm. A creeping or sprawling herb. Leaves appear 3-lobed, although with two extra leaflets at base of stalk. Long pods spread out like a bird's foot. Fl 5–9; Md, Pa; P.

KIDNEY VETCH
Anthyllis vulneraria
H 10–30cm. A creeping or upright herb. Leaves covered with silky hairs, flowers yellow, in heads, with distinctive, woolly sepals. Fl 5–9; Mt, C, Pa; P.

HARE'S-FOOT CLOVER
Trifolium arvense
H 5–20cm. An erect, hairy herb. Leaves 3-lobed, with narrow leaflets. Flowers pinkish, in dense heads, with silky-haired sepals. Fl 6–9; C, F, Pa; A or B.

CRANESBILLS AND STORKSBILLS

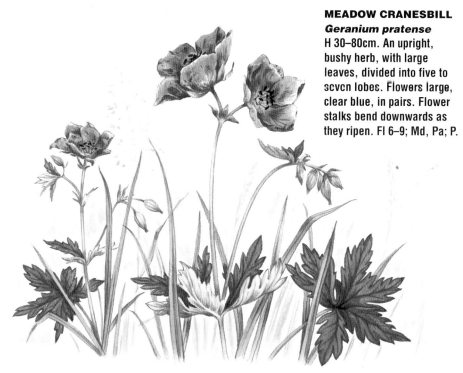

MEADOW CRANESBILL
Geranium pratense
H 30–80cm. An upright, bushy herb, with large leaves, divided into five to seven lobes. Flowers large, clear blue, in pairs. Flower stalks bend downwards as they ripen. Fl 6–9; Md, Pa; P.

GENERAL FEATURES

The cranesbills and storksbills all have colourful, regular flowers, with five separate petals and ten stamens. Their fruits are distinctively beak-shaped, splitting, when ripe, into five parts. The cranesbills have lobed leaves, whilst the storksbills have leaves divided into pairs of leaflets. Wood sorrel comes from a closely-related family, with three-lobed leaves and less distinctive fruits.

HABITATS

Cranesbills and storksbills grow in many different, usually sunny, habitats. The best places to see them include meadows, clearings in woodland, roadsides and old walls. Storksbills prefer coastal areas.

Two other widespread species might be confused with meadow cranesbill: wood cranesbill has more purplish-blue flowers that do not open as wide, and the fruit is held erect. Bloody cranesbill (above) has deep-red flowers and is usually slightly smaller.

COMMON STORKSBILL
Erodium cicutarium
H to 30cm. Spreading or ascending, sticky-haired herb. Leaves divided into pairs of leaflets, with each leaflet divided again. Pink flowers, often with dark spots. Fl 6–9; C, Pa; A or B.

◬ DOVE'S FOOT CRANESBILL
Geranium molle
H 10–40cm. Hairy, spreading herb. Leaves divided to about halfway. Flowers pink, with notched petals and ten pink anthers. Fl 5–9; F, W; A.

HERB ROBERT ▷
Geranium robertianum
H 10–40cm. Erect or spreading, strongly scented herb. Leaves shiny green, hairy. Flowers pink, with orange or purple stamens. Fl 5–9; C, Wa, Wd; A.

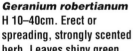

WOOD SORREL ◬
Oxalis acetosella
H 5–12cm. Creeping herb, with 3-lobed leaves. Single white flowers streaked with lilac. Fl 4–5; Wd; P.

HOW TO FIND

Wood sorrel is one of a small group of plants that tend to grow only in ancient woodland i.e. woodland that has been around for hundreds of years. Such plants fail to spread into newer woodland. Try looking at old maps, or look for woods with old banks and ditches around them. Wood sorrel likes acid soil, especially under beech trees.

BALSAMS AND OTHERS

GENERAL FEATURES

The plants shown here come from several, related families. Most have strange and rather distinctive flowers. The balsams have large, irregular, helmet-shaped flowers, with a long spur on the lower sepal. Spurges have inconspicuous but bizarre flowers, with globe-shaped ovaries and large, rounded or crescent-shaped glands; male and female flowers are quite separate. The milkworts have small, attractive flowers, with three petals fused into a tube, and two sepals enlarged into colourful, petal-like wings. The flaxes have simple, regular, five-petalled flowers. These plants can be found in a variety of different habitats.

There are three other types of balsam besides Himalayan balsam, all with yellow-orange flowers. The common name of this one is 'touch-me-not', referring to the way in which the ripe capsules explode if touched.

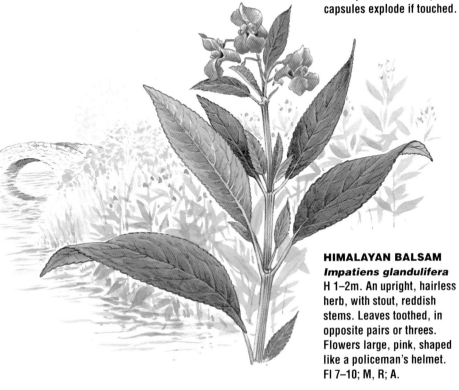

HIMALAYAN BALSAM
Impatiens glandulifera
H 1–2m. An upright, hairless herb, with stout, reddish stems. Leaves toothed, in opposite pairs or threes. Flowers large, pink, shaped like a policeman's helmet.
Fl 7–10; M, R; A.

SUN SPURGE 🌾
Euphorbia helioscopia
H 10–30cm. A hairless, upright, unbranched herb, with a ring of five, oval bracts below the five main branches of the flower cluster. Fl 5–8; F, W; A.

DOG'S MERCURY 🔺
Mercurialis perennis
H 15–40cm. Upright, hairy plant with creeping, underground stem. Male and female flowers on separate plants. Fl 3–4; Wd, Mt; P.

FAIRY FLAX 🔺
Linum catharticum
H 5–25cm. An upright, slender, hairless plant. Leaves oblong, greyish, in pairs. Flowers small, white, in drooping clusters. Fl 5–9; Mt, Md, Pa; A or B.

PROJECT

When ripe, the capsules of Himalayan balsam explode if touched, scattering the seeds everywhere. Try finding out how far the furthest seeds are flung, and when you have collected a few, test them to see if they float on water. This reveals the secret of the plant's success along river banks.

COMMON MILKWORT
Polygala vulgaris
H 5–15cm. A small, hairless, upright herb. Leaves alternate, narrow, pointed. Flowers blue, pink, white or mauve. Fl 5–7; Md, Pa, Mt; P.

MALLOWS AND OTHERS

COMMON MALLOW
Malva sylvestris
H 45–90cm. An upright or spreading, branched herb. Leaves alternate, divided to less than halfway. Flowers about 2.5cm across, rose-pink with darker veins, in clusters. Fl 6–9; F, Pa; P.

GENERAL FEATURES

The mallow family are a very attractive group of flowers. They include a number of garden plants, such as hollyhocks, as well as economically important plants like cotton. The flowers have five separate petals and sepals, often with an extra outer whorl of leaves outside the sepals. Normally, the flowers are pink or red. The fruit consists of a ring of tightly-packed seeds in a saucer-like structure. The violet and pansy family have distinctive and well-known flowers, with five irregular petals.

HABITATS

All the flowers shown here are plants of open, sunny habitats, such as roadsides, limestone grassland or cultivated land.

'Bread and cheese'
Plants have scientific names because common names can be very confusing. Mallow, for example, has many local names, including 'bread and cheese', 'flibberty gibbet', 'horse button', 'pancake plant', and 'rags and tatters'. It would be impossible to learn all the names and, in many cases, one name can refer to two different plants.

MUSK MALLOW
Malva moschata
H 30–80cm. An upright herb. Stem leaves deeply divided into narrow segments; base leaves 3-lobed. Flowers pink. Fl 7–8; F, Pa; P.

WILD PANSY
Viola tricolor
H 5–15cm. Upright, spreading or tufted herb. Leaves narrow, flowers yellow, bluish, or both. Fl 5–10; C, F, W; A or P.

COMMON ST JOHN'S WORT
Hypericum perforatum
H 30–90cm. An upright herb. Leaves oval, with many transparent glands. Flowers yellow, with black dots on petals. Fl 6–8; F, Pa; P.

COMMON ROCKROSE
Helianthemum nummularium
H 5–30cm. A creeping shrub, with upright flowering stems from a woody stem. Leaves small, opposite. Flowers yellow, to 2.5cm across, with red-striped sepals. Fl 5–7; Pa, Md; P.

COMMON DOG VIOLET
Viola riviniana
H 5–20cm. A hairless herb, with heart-shaped leaves in a rosette. Flowers violet, with a broad, whitish spur behind. Fl 3–5; Mt, Wd, Pa; P.

WILLOWHERBS AND OTHERS

PURPLE LOOSESTRIFE
Lythrum salicaria
H 60–120cm. An upright,
downy herb, with narrow,
oval leaves, opposite or in
whorls of three. Flowers
purple, about 1.5cm across,
in whorls up the stem, with 6
petals and 12 stamens.
Fl 7–8; M; P.

GENERAL FEATURES

The willowherb family is a rather variable
group, with flower parts in twos or fours and
twice as many stamens as petals. The
willowherbs themselves all have pinkish flowers
and silky, wind-distributed seeds, but the
enchanter's nightshades, although in the same
family, have white flowers and fruits with
hooked bristles. Purple loosestrife, although
similar, is in a different family, with usually 6
petals and 12 stamens. White bryony is quite
different, the only North European member of
the cucumber family. It has greenish flowers,
red, fleshy berries and tendrils from the stem.

The other common name for
rosebay willowherb is
fireweed. This is because it
quickly appears on burnt
areas and bomb sites,
turning them rose-coloured
with its haze of flowers. It
colonises new, suitable
areas very quickly with its
numerous, downy, wind-
borne seeds.

ENCHANTER'S NIGHTSHADE ▷
Circaea lutetiana
H 20–70cm. A herb, with creeping roots and upright, flowering stems. Leaves oval, in opposite pairs. Pinkish-white flowers in long spikes. Fruit rounded, with hooked bristles. Fl 6–8; F, Wd; P.

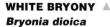

WHITE BRYONY ▲
Bryonia dioica
H up to 4m. A scrambling or climbing herb, with bristly stems and long tendrils growing from leaf bases. Male and female flowers separate, greenish-white. Fl 5–8; F, Wd; P.

GREAT WILLOWHERB
Epilobium hirsutum
H 60–150cm. An erect, very hairy herb, with rounded stems. Leaves in pairs, clasping the stem. Flowers pinkish-purple, about 2cm across, with a 4-lobed white stigma. Fl 7–8; M, Md; P.

ROSEBAY WILLOWHERB ▷
Chamerion angustifolium
H 50–120cm. An upright herb, with spirally-arranged, narrow leaves. Flowers deep rose, with two upper petals broader than lower. Fl 6–9; F, W; P.

FLOWERS WITH UMBELS 1

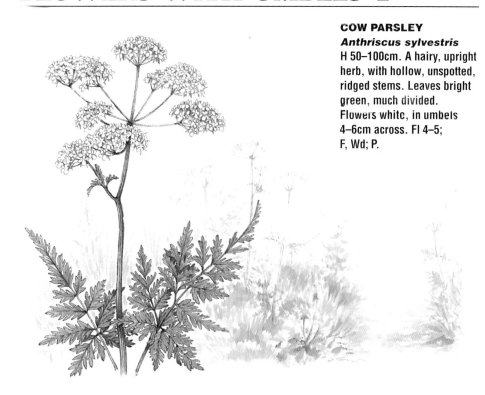

COW PARSLEY
Anthriscus sylvestris
H 50–100cm. A hairy, upright
herb, with hollow, unspotted,
ridged stems. Leaves bright
green, much divided.
Flowers white, in umbels
4–6cm across. Fl 4–5;
F, Wd; P.

GENERAL FEATURES

The carrot family, or *Umbelliferae*, all have
flowers arranged in umbels – like the spokes of
an upside-down umbrella. Often each ray of the
umbel has another smaller umbel on it, making
a compound umbel, with numerous flowers. Ivy
is in a closely related family and also has umbels
of flowers, but its fruits are round and fleshy.

HABITATS

Cow parsley is commonly found on roadside
verges, where its masses of white flowers are a
familiar sight in spring. Wood sanicle is most
likely to be found in old woodlands, while sea
holly grows mainly on sand dunes. Ivy and
ground elder are common almost everywhere.

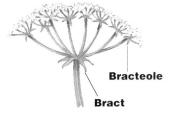

Bracteole

Bract

There are many similar-
looking plants in this family.
One of the important things
to look for is the presence
and shape of bracts and
bracteoles. Bracts are little
leaf-like structures that can
be found at the base of the
main umbel rays, while
bracteoles grow at the base
of the secondary rays.

GROUND ELDER
Aegopodium podagraria
H 40–100cm. An upright, creeping, hairless herb, forming large patches. Leaves 3-lobed, often divided again. Flowers white, in heads to 6cm across. Fl 5–8; F, W; P.

IVY
Hedera helix
H from ground to tree-tops. Climbing/scrambling plant, clinging on to walls or trees by fine rootlets. Dark green, lobed leaves and simple umbels of greenish flowers. Fl 9–11; C, F, Wd; P.

SANICLE
Sanicula europaea
H 20–60cm. An upright, hairless herb. Long-stalked, divided leaves at base. Flowers pink or white, fruit bristly. Fl 5–6; Wd; P.

SEA HOLLY
Eryngium maritimum
H 25–60cm. An upright, branched, hairless, spiny plant, with grey-green, waxy leaves. Flowers purplish, in simple umbels with spiny bracts. Fl 6–9; C; P.

FLOWERS WITH UMBELS 2

GENERAL FEATURES

The plants shown here, with the exception of common wintergreen, also have umbels of flowers like the species on pp.80–81. The wintergreens are a small group of flowers with a rosette of slightly waxy, undivided leaves, and spikes of bell-shaped, usually drooping, pink or white flowers. Most of them are rare, although common wintergreen, as its name suggests, is more widespread.

HABITATS

Many of these plants are generally found in open, grassy areas. Angelica and giant hogweed grow in wet places, while wild carrot thrives in dry, chalky soil, especially near the coast. Wintergreen grows mainly in woods.

Several of our familiar vegetables, such as parsnip and carrot, have been developed from wild plants of this family. When we eat root vegetables, such as carrots, we are actually eating the food store collected by a biennial plant in preparation for flowering in its second year.

ANGELICA
Angelica sylvestris
H 50–200cm. A tall, stout, upright herb, with hollow purplish stems. Leaves much divided, triangular in outline. Flowers white or pink, in large, round umbels.
Fl 7–8; M, Md; P.

HOGWEED
Heracleum sphondylium
H 50–200cm. An upright, rough-haired plant with hollow stems. Leaves greyish-green with toothed lobes. Flowers white, in large heads, outer flowers largest. Fl 5–9; M, F, Wd; B.

WILD CARROT
Daucus carota
H 25–100cm. Upright, rough-haired plant. Leaves fern-like. Umbels with fern-like bracts. Fl 6–8; C, Pa; B.

COMMON WINTERGREEN
Pyrola minor
H 10-30cm. Small evergreen plant, with rosette of stalked, light green, oval leaves, and central spike of drooping, pink-white flowers. Fl 6–7; Mt, C, Wd; P.

PROJECT

Giant hogweed, probably the largest herbaceous plant in western Europe, grows very quickly. If you have some near you, try working out its growth rate by measuring its height each month (be careful not to rub against the plant in sunny weather, because it can cause blisters on your skin).

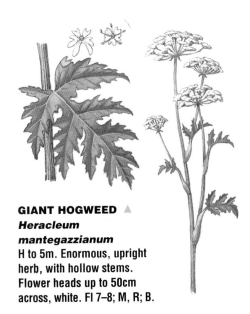

GIANT HOGWEED
Heracleum mantegazzianum
H to 5m. Enormous, upright herb, with hollow stems. Flower heads up to 50cm across, white. Fl 7–8; M, R; B.

THE HEATHER FAMILY

GENERAL FEATURES

The heather family is mainly made up of low-growing shrubs with woody stems. They are commonly evergreen and often have very small leaves. The flowers have four or five parts, and the petals are joined into a tube. The heathers themselves have dry fruits and seeds, but other members of the family, such as bilberry or cranberry, have fleshy, edible fruits.

HABITATS

Members of the heather family (which includes the rhododendrons) grow best on acid soils. Ling, bell heather and bilberry are usually found on drier soils, whilst cranberry and cross-leaved heath live in wet areas with acidic soil, particularly in bogs.

The three most common heathers are described here, but there are also a few less widespread species that are worth looking out for. Dorset heath has long spikes of deep pink flowers and is found in southwest England and Ireland. Cornish heath (above) has masses of small, white or lilac flowers. This heather is found in Cornwall and also in Ireland.

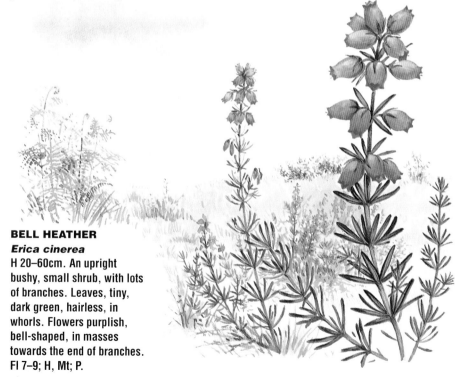

BELL HEATHER
Erica cinerea
H 20–60cm. An upright bushy, small shrub, with lots of branches. Leaves, tiny, dark green, hairless, in whorls. Flowers purplish, bell-shaped, in masses towards the end of branches.
Fl 7–9; H, Mt; P.

CROSS-LEAVED HEATH
Erica tetralix
H 10–30cm. A low shrub,
smaller than bell heather,
with hairy branches. Leaves
greyish, flowers rose-pink.
Fl 6–10; H, M; P.

BILBERRY
Vaccinium myrtillus
H 20–60cm. A hairless shrub,
with small, oval leaves and
green stems. Flowers pink,
later producing purplish-
black berries. Fl 4–5;
H, Mt; P.

CRANBERRY
Vaccinium oxycoccus
H up to 8cm. Low, creeping
shrub, with slender stems
and tiny leaves. Pink flowers
on thin stalks, with a column
of stamens. Fl 6–7; M; P.

PROJECT

On heathlands, it is known that gorse
tends to grow where the soil has been
disturbed. The disturbance may not be
a new one – it could have happened a
long time ago, perhaps even in
prehistoric times. Gorse bushes may
therefore mark the sites of ancient
features, Try matching up patches of
gorse with the archaeological sites
marked on a good map, and see what
you find.

LING
Calluna vulgaris
H 30–60cm. Small, bushy
shrub with pink flowers and
tiny leaves. Fl 7–9; H,
Mt, M; P.

THE PRIMROSE FAMILY

GENERAL FEATURES

Primroses and cowslips are familiar members of the primrose family, although it is surprising what other flowers are in the same family. They are all herbs, with leaves that do not have stipules. The flowers are regular, with the petals joined together into a tube, and the free parts spreading out to a greater or lesser extent. In cyclamen (not shown here), this is not obvious because the petals bend right back, making the flower look quite different. There are the same number of stamens as there are petals (usually five), the stamens being attached to the tube part of the petals. The family as a whole includes many attractive garden plants such as primulas and polyanthus.

Thrum-eyed   Pin-eyed

Primroses have two different types of flowers; in the pin-eyed type, the style is visible at the tips of the petals and the stamens are hidden. In the thrum-eyed type, the stamens are visible while the style is hidden.

PRIMROSE
Primula vulgaris
H to 15cm. A small herb, with rosettes of spoon-shaped, wrinkled leaves, From these grow hairy stems, bearing single, yellow flowers. Fl 3–5; Wd, Pa; P.

CHICKWEED WINTERGREEN ▽
Trientalis europaea
H 10–25cm. A slender, upright herb, with a single ruff of oval leaves and starry, white flowers. Despite its name, this plant is neither a chickweed nor a wintergreen. Fl 6–7; Wd, Mt; P.

SCARLET PIMPERNEL ▲
Anagallis arvensis
H very low, up to 30cm long. A spreading, hairless herb, with pairs of oval leaves. Flowers orange-red (rarely blue). Fl 5–10; F, W; A.

YELLOW PIMPERNEL ▲
Lysimachia nemorum
H very low, up to 50cm long. A creeping herb, with opposite pairs of pointed leaves and single, yellow flowers. Fl 5–7; Wd; P.

COWSLIP ▲
Primula veris
H 10–30cm. A hairy, upright herb, with rosette of stalked leaves, and single stems bearing umbels of yellow flowers. Fl 4–5; Md, Pa; P.

◄ YELLOW LOOSESTRIFE
Lysimachia vulgaris
H 60–150cm. An upright, hairy herb, with leaves in pairs or whorls, dotted with black. Flowers bright yellow, 1.5cm across, in branched clusters. Fl 7–8; M, R, Md; P.

THRIFT AND GENTIANS

THRIFT
Armeria maritima
H 10–30cm. A cushion-forming plant with woody, spreading roots and numerous, very narrow leaves. Flowers in rounded heads on leafless stalks. Fl 4–6; C, Mt; P.

GENERAL FEATURES

A motley collection of flowers from three different families. Thrift is in the sea-lavender family, with flowers divided into five parts, and paper-like sepals. Felwort and centaury both belong to the gentian family and have flowers with four or five petals, joined below into a tube. Periwinkle comes from a closely related family – the periwinkle family – in which the petal lobes spread out like a wheel, and all the petals are twisted together in the bud. The periwinkle family includes many examples of both poisonous plants and plants used as medicines, although only two species (lesser and greater periwinkle) regularly occur in Britain and northern Europe.

Thrift is one of a small group of plants that thrive on the coast and on mountain tops, but hardly anywhere else. It survives on difficult ground with the help of its long roots, which can reach good water supplies some way below the surface. Thrift can also grow on salty soil.

LESSER PERIWINKLE
Vinca minor
H to 20cm. Creeping,
evergreen shrub, forming
large patches. Leaves oval,
pointed, shiny, dark green, in
opposite pairs. Wheel-
shaped flowers are blue-
violet with white ring around
centre. Fl 4–5; Wd, F; P.

PROJECT

FELWORT
Gentianella amarella
H 5–35cm. An upright herb,
with opposite, pointed leaves
and clusters of erect, bell-
shaped, pinkish flowers. The
'throat' of each flower is
fringed with white hairs.
Fl 7–9; Pa, C, Mt; B.

A plum has just one seed inside it,
while an orchid capsule may contain
100,000 seeds, yet both types of plant
survive and spread. Try investigating a
selection of flowers and counting the
number of seeds per plant to see how
much they vary (for those with lots of
seeds, like foxgloves, just make an
estimate using a small sample). Try to
work out whether there is any
relationship between number of seeds
and type of plant.

COMMON CENTAURY
Centaurium erythraea
H 10–40cm. An upright herb,
with a rosette of spoon-
shaped leaves, and one or
more stems bearing
branched clusters of pink
flowers. Fl 6–9; Pa, C, Wd; A.

BINDWEEDS AND BEDSTRAWS

GENERAL FEATURES

The bindweeds are well-known and distinctive plants, and frequent garden weeds. They are mainly climbing plants, twining around other vegetation. The leaves are alternate, and the flowers have five petals fused into a trumpet-shape, with five sepals outside. The bedstraws are quite different, with distinctive whorls of leaves and small, tube-shaped flowers.

HABITATS

The two bindweeds, and goose grass, are weeds of disturbed ground, field edges and similar places. Lady's bedstraw is a plant of more stable grassland, such as downs or old sand dunes, never occurring as a weed.

It is a curious fact that all bindweed plants twine around their supporting plant in the same direction – anti-clockwise – however they start off. Look at a few examples, then check any other climbing plants you can find to see what they do.

HEDGE BINDWEED
Calystegia sepium
H to 3m. A vigorous, climbing plant, also known as bellbine. Leaves oval, heart-shaped at base. Large, white, trumpet-shaped flowers, to 5cm across. FI 6–9; F, W; P.

FIELD BINDWEED ▲
Convolvulus arvensis
H 20–75cm. A climbing and
scrambling herb, with long,
twining stems. Leaves
alternate, arrow-shaped.
Flowers white, pink, or
mixed. Fl 6–9; F, W; P.

LADY'S BEDSTRAW ▲
Galium verum
H 20–60cm. Creeping or
erect herb, with whorls of
narrow, dark green leaves
and dense clusters of yellow
flowers. Fl 6–8; C, Md, Pa; P.

GOOSEGRASS ▲
Galium aparine
H to over 1m long. A
scrambling plant, supporting
itself on other vegetation
with its prickles. Flowers
greenish-white, small.
Fl 5–9; F, Wa, C, Wd; A.

HOW TO FIND

Many types of similar plants cross-
breed, or hybridise, to produce
individuals which look slightly
different from both parents. For
example, primrose and cowslip
hybridise to produce the pale
yellow-flowered false oxlip, shown
here. To find hybrids, look for
unusual-looking plants in places
where both parents grow close
together.

FORGET-ME-NOTS AND OTHERS

GENERAL FEATURES

The forget-me-not, or borage, family consists of herbaceous (non-woody) plants that are almost all bristly or very hairy, with alternate leaves, and flowers in clusters. The flowers themselves have five parts, with petals fused into a tube and five separate lobes. Bugle is a member of the dead-nettle family (see pp.94–95).

HABITATS

Viper's bugloss is a plant of sand dunes, other coastal habitats, and dry, grassy areas. Wood forget-me-not, as the name suggests, occurs most commonly in woodlands, while field forget-me-not is more a plant of disturbed ground and dry, open areas. Comfrey is often found along the sides of rivers and in marshes.

Comfrey is one of the main food plants for scarlet tiger moths. These beautiful moths show their scarlet underwings mainly in flight. They occur in marshy areas where there is plenty of comfrey for them to eat.

VIPER'S BUGLOSS
Echium vulgare
H 30–90cm. An upright plant, with lots of red-based bristles up the stem. Leaves mainly in a rosette. Flowers in numerous, short, side branches, forming a long spike altogether.
Fl 6–8; C, Pa; B.

FIELD FORGET-ME-NOT
Myosotis arvensis
H 15–35cm. An upright, hairy herb, with tongue-shaped leaves. Flowers tiny, blue, in short, curving clusters. Fl 4–6; F, W; A or B.

BUGLE
Ajuga reptans
H to 20cm. A creeping plant with leafy runners, producing upright, flowering stems. Stems square, hairy on two sides, with leafy whorls of blue-purple flowers. Fl 4–6; Mt, Wd, Md, Pa; P.

WOOD FORGET-ME-NOT
Myosotis sylvatica
H 15–40cm. An upright plant, rather like field forget-me-not, but often larger, with brighter blue flowers 6–10mm across. Fl 4–6; Wd, Md; P.

COMMON COMFREY
Symphytum officinale
H 50–100cm. An upright, brIstly herb, with winged stems. Flowers in coiled clusters, usually yellowish-white, sometimes pink. Fl 4–6; M, Md; P.

WOOD SAGE
Teucrium scorodonia
H 15–60cm. A hairy, upright plant, with crinkly, strong-smelling leaves. Flowers small, greenish-yellow, with red stamens. Fl 7–9; Wd; P.

THE DEAD-NETTLE FAMILY 1

YELLOW ARCHANGEL
Lamiastrum galeobdolon
H 20–60cm. A herb with long, creeping, leafy runners, producing upright, flowering stems with oval leaves. Flowers yellow with orange markings, arranged in whorls up the stem. Fl 4–6; Wd; P.

GENERAL FEATURES

The dead-nettles are so-called because many of them have leaves like stinging nettles, but they have no sting. The main characteristics of this large family are the square stems, opposite leaves, and whorls of irregular flowers. Many species are strong-smelling, and they often contain essential oils. Herbs such as thyme, marjoram, basil and mint come from this family.

HABITATS

Yellow archangel is a plant of woodlands and hedgebanks, whilst red dead-nettle, white dead-nettle, and hemp-nettle are all plants of waste or disturbed ground, often becoming weeds in gardens and on farmland.

The larger dead-nettle flowers are ideal for visiting honey bees and bumble bees. The large flower lip acts as a landing platform, and the nectar at the base of the petal tube is easy to get at. In reaching for this, the bees pick up pollen to transfer to the next flower they visit.

RED DEAD-NETTLE ▶

Lamium purpureum
H 10–30cm. An upright, hairy
herb, branched from the
base, with reddish stems and
leaves. Leaves and bracts
(below the flowers) pointed,
toothed and stalked. Flowers
red, in heads at the top of the
stems. Fl 3–12; F, W; A.

WHITE DEAD-NETTLE ▼

Lamium album
H 20–60cm. An upright,
hairy, tufted plant, with
leaves very like stinging
nettle, but without the sting.
Large, white flowers with
arched top petals, arranged
in whorls near the stem tops.
Fl 4–6; F, W, Wd, Md; P.

◀ COMMON HEMP-NETTLE

Galeopsis tetrahit
H 20–80cm. An upright,
branching plant, with sticky
hairs. Stem swollen at the
joints, leaves oval, pointed
and toothed. Flowers pink or
white, with purple markings.
Fl 5–8; F, Wd, Md; A.

HOW TO FIND

Yellow archangel is a plant of
woods and older hedgerows,
especially on heavy soils (such as
clay) or on soils rich in lime. It
does particularly well in ancient
woodland and may become
abundant in the right conditions.
Use a geological map to find out
what kinds of rocks there are in a
region – these should be available
in local libraries. Look for areas of
chalk, limestone or clay, and then
check older-looking woods or
hedgerows.

THE DEAD-NETTLE FAMILY 2

GENERAL FEATURES

All the flowers shown here are in the dead-nettle family, sharing the characteristics of the plants on pp.94–95; all have square stems, whorls of irregular flowers, and are generally fragrant or strong-smelling.

HABITATS

Betony is found on dry banks and in woodland clearings, on both acid soil and soil rich in lime. Hedge woundwort, which can look rather similar, and ground ivy prefer slightly more disturbed conditions such as hedgebanks, woodland edges, and even gardens. Thyme and selfheal are both flowers of open sunny places and will grow in various types of soil.

More mints
Water mint, shown here, is probably the commonest mint, but there are many other types, both wild and cultivated, each with a different smell and taste. Spearmint is well-known, but there is also apple mint, scented of apple, horse mint (not very good to eat) and many others. There are also numerous crossbreeds, or hybrids, producing new scents and tastes. One example is peppermint, a cross between watermint and spearmint.

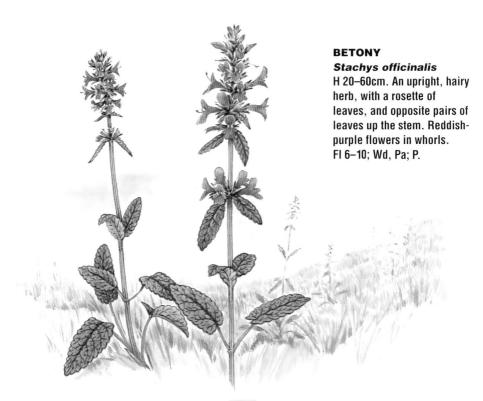

BETONY
Stachys officinalis
H 20–60cm. An upright, hairy herb, with a rosette of leaves, and opposite pairs of leaves up the stem. Reddish-purple flowers in whorls.
Fl 6–10; Wd, Pa; P.

WATER MINT
Mentha aquatica
H 15–60cm. An upright, hairy herb, with opposite pairs of oval leaves that smell strongly of mint, and pink flowers. Fl 7–9; M, Md; P.

HEDGE WOUNDWORT
Stachys sylvatica
H 30–80cm. An upright, bad-smelling herb with creeping stems. Triangular, toothed leaves and wine-red flowers in whorls at the top of the stem. Fl 6–9; F, Wd; P.

WILD THYME
Thymus praecox
H up to 15cm. A low, creeping plant, with oval leaves and purplish flowers. Strongly-scented, like thyme. Fl 6–9; Mt, C, Pa; P.

GROUND IVY
Glechoma hederacea
H to 20cm. A creeping, strong-smelling, hairy plant with stalked, kidney-shaped leaves. Whorls of violet flowers grow from the points where the leaves join the stem. Fl 4–6; F, Wd; P.

SELFHEAL
Prunella vulgaris
H 5–20cm. Hairy herb with erect, flowering stems. Leaves oval, opposite, flowers violet (sometimes white), in short, oblong heads at the stem tips. Fl 4–7; F, W, Wd, Md, Pa; P.

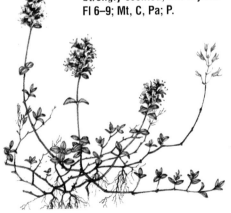

NIGHTSHADES AND FIGWORTS

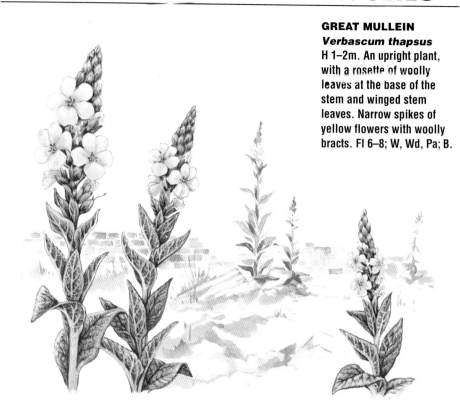

GREAT MULLEIN
Verbascum thapsus
H 1–2m. An upright plant, with a rosette of woolly leaves at the base of the stem and winged stem leaves. Narrow spikes of yellow flowers with woolly bracts. Fl 6–8; W, Wd, Pa; B.

GENERAL FEATURES

The nightshades belong to the large, mainly tropical, potato family which contains a strange mixture of highly-poisonous and very edible plants. Potato, tomato, Cape gooseberry and other familiar crop plants are in this family. The flowers are symmetrical and have five parts, with the lower part of the petals fused into a tube. In some species, the five stamens stick out in a column. The fruits of all wild nightshades are poisonous, however edible they may look. Mullein and monkey flower are both members of the very large figwort or foxglove family (see pp.100–101).

One of the ways that you can tell different species of mullein apart is by looking at their stamens. Some, like great mullein, have white hairs on some of their stamens; others, like dark mullein (above) have purple hairs on all their stamens.

WOODY NIGHTSHADE
Solanum dulcamara
H to 2m. A scrambling plant with purple flowers. Each flower has five turned-back petal lobes, and a cone of bright yellow stamens. Fl 6–9; M, F, W, Wd; P.

MONKEY FLOWER
Mimulus guttatus
H 20–50cm. An upright herb with creeping roots and oval, toothed leaves. Yellow flowers marked with tiny, red dots. Fl 6–7; M, R, Md; P.

DEADLY NIGHTSHADE
Atropa belladonna
H 50–150cm. An upright, bushy herb. Purple, bell-shaped, flowers; berries black, large and very poisonous. Fl 7–8; Wd, W; P.

PROJECT

It is a common sight to see a wall covered with flowering plants. But have you ever wondered how they got there, or how they manage to survive in such difficult conditions? You might expect any seeds produced by the plants above to fall straight to the ground. To see what really happens, take a look at a few wall plants when they are producing fruits towards the end of summer. If a real wall specialist like ivy-leaved toadflax (see p.101) is present, look at it carefully. You will notice that its stalks start to grow in a different direction as the fruits begin to ripen. They slowly curve round to eventually push the seed capsules into the wall cracks.

THE FIGWORT FAMILY 2

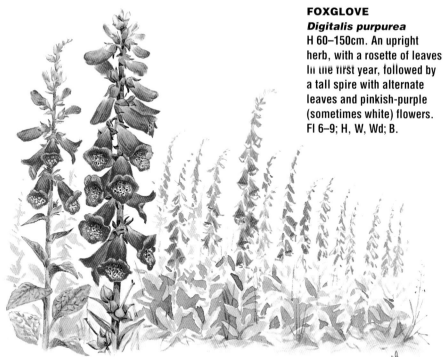

FOXGLOVE
Digitalis purpurea
H 60–150cm. An upright
herb, with a rosette of leaves
in the first year, followed by
a tall spire with alternate
leaves and pinkish-purple
(sometimes white) flowers.
Fl 6–9; H, W, Wd; B.

GENERAL FEATURES

The figwort, or foxglove, family is very large,
with many different species in North Europe.
These plants are very similar to the members of
the dead-nettle family, differing mainly in the
shape and form of the fruit. The flowers usually
have parts in fives, with the petals joined into a
tube, spreading out into two main lobes.

HABITATS

Foxglove is a plant of waste ground, waysides,
forest clearings, and other temporarily clear
areas, often being highly successful for a few
years, then fading away. This is typical of
biennial plants (plants that grow from seed and
form a plant in one year, then flower and die in
the following year).

a   **b**

To accurately identify one of
the many species of
speedwell, you need to look
closely at details such as
flower arrangement. Wood
speedwell, for example, (a)
grows spikes of flowers from
the points where the leaves
join the stem, whilst thyme-
leaved speedwell (b) bears
single flowers from the
bases of the leaves.

COMMON FIGWORT
Scrophularia nodosa
H 40–80cm. An upright, almost hairless herb, with pairs of oval, toothed leaves. Stems square, with sticky hairs. Flowers green and red. Fl 6–8; F, Wd; P.

IVY-LEAVED TOADFLAX
Cymbalaria muralis
H to 20cm long. A creeping or spreading, hairless plant, with long-stalked, ivy-shaped leaves. Lilac flowers, about 1cm long, with a yellow centre and short spur. Fl 6–9; F, W; P.

BIRD'S EYE SPEEDWELL
Veronica chamaedrys
H 10–20cm. A creeping or semi-upright herb. Stem has two rows of long white hairs. Fl 5–7, F, Wd; P.

COMMON TOADFLAX
Linaria vulgaris
H 30–80cm. An upright, grey-green, almost hairless plant, with a rosette of narrow leaves, and alternate leaves up the stem. Flowers yellow with an orange centre, in spikes at the top of stems. Fl 7–8; F, W, Wd, Pa; P.

HEATH SPEEDWELL
Veronica officinalis
H 10–15cm. A creeping, hairy plant, with upright spikes of pale, blue-lilac flowers, each about 6mm across. Fl 5–8; H, Pa; P.

THE FIGWORT FAMILY 3

YELLOW RATTLE
Rhinanthus minor
H 20–50cm. An upright, hairless herb, with a square, black-spotted stem. Leaves narrow, oval, toothed, in opposite pairs. Flowers yellow, with two violet 'teeth', in short, leafy spikes. Sepals swell up in fruit, and the seeds rattle inside.
Fl 6–7; Md, Pa; A.

GENERAL FEATURES

These plants share the same general characteristics as those described for this family on p.100. However, this particular group of plants share one additional feature – they are all semi-parasites. They all have ordinary leaves and can make their own food from sunlight, as other plants do. But they can also 'tap in' to the roots of nearby plants, to steal food from them and to weaken their growth so that there is less competition. In places where there are a lot of these plants around, the effect on the surrounding vegetation is usually quite obvious. They are all most common on grasslands or in damp, open places.

Bright eyes
In the past, people believed that if a plant looked like a part of the human body, it could be used to cure disease in that part of the body. Eyebright, with its 'bright-eyed' flowers, was once used to help cure eye troubles and improve poor eyesight. In fact, an extract from eyebright plants is still used in the preparation of certain eye lotions.

EYEBRIGHT
Euphrasia officinalis
H 10–20cm. An upright, slender herb, often purplish-green. Leaves opposite, deeply toothed. Flowers small, white, with orange centre and purplish lines on petals. Fl 6–8; Mt, H, Pa; A.

RED BARTSIA
Odontites verna
H 10–50cm. An upright, branching, hairy herb. Leaves opposite, slightly toothed. Flowers pink, with two-lipped petal tube. Fl 7–10; F, W, Md, Pa; A.

COMMON COW-WHEAT
Melampyrum pratense
H 10–40cm. An upright or spreading, almost hairless plant, with opposite pairs of leaves. Pairs of pale yellow flowers, both turned to one side. Fl 7–8; M, Wd; A.

LOUSEWORT
Pedicularis sylvatica
H 10–20cm. Low herb, with deeply divided leaves and upright, pink flowers in a cluster at the top of stem. Shorter than similar red rattle, and flowers earlier. Fl 5–7; Mt, M, Pa; P.

RED RATTLE
Pedicularis palustris
H 20–60cm. Similar to, but taller than lousewort, with flowers spread further along stem; plant often reddish. Upper lip of petal tube has four teeth. Fl 6–8; M, Md; A.

BROOMRAPES AND PLANTAINS

GENERAL FEATURES

The broomrapes are total parasites. They take all their food from another species of plant, known as their host plant. Most species of broomrape will only take food from one small group of host plants, although common broomrape is not so fussy. The plantains are distinctive for the rosettes of leaves at their base and their long spikes of tiny flowers on leafless stems.

HABITATS

Common broomrape, and the two plantains shown here, are plants of cultivated and disturbed ground, although broomrape is limited to the places where its host plants (mainly clovers and cultivated beans and peas) grow. Honeysuckle grows best on acid soils.

Toothwort is closely related to broomrape and quite similar. However, it has pink rather than yellow flowers, in a one-sided spike on a pink or white stem. Toothwort is parasitic on woody plants such as hazel and maple, growing mainly on chalky soils. Its flowers appear early in spring.

COMMON BROOMRAPE
Orobanche minor
H 10–50cm. An upright, hairy plant, with leaves reduced to brownish scales. Spikes of yellow flowers, often tinged purple. Fl 5–7; F, W, Pa; P.

RIBWORT PLANTAIN ▲
Plantago lanceolata
H 10–40cm. Herb, with rosette of narrow leaves. Leafless, hairy stems bear spikes of greenish-brown flowers with white stamens. Fl 4–10; F, W, Md, Pa; P.

GREATER PLANTAIN ▲
Plantago major
H 10–40cm. Similar to ribwort plantain, but with much broader, oval, hairless leaves, and long thin flower spikes, to 8cm long. Fl 6–10; F, W; P.

HONEYSUCKLE ▲
Lonicera periclymenum
H to 6m. A climbing,woody plant, reaching high up on other vegetation. Leaves opposite, oval, dense heads of fragrant, yellowish-pink flowers. Fl 6–8; F, Wd; P.

HOW TO FIND

Broomrapes, which include many of our rarest plants, are commonest in the south. To look for them, you need to know which plants they take their food from (their host plants). Look amongst gorse and broom for greater broomrape or amongst greater knapweed for tall broomrape, which occurs mainly on chalk. Ivy has its own broomrape (shown here), and this is best searched for in limestone areas, especially near the coast.

BELLFLOWERS AND OTHERS

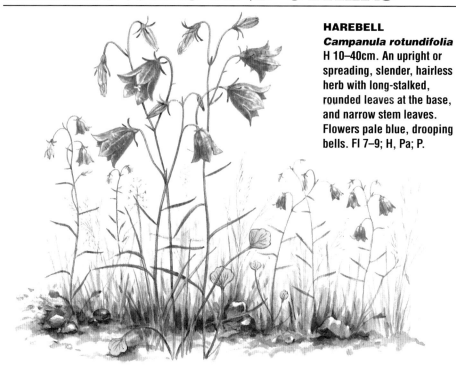

HAREBELL
Campanula rotundifolia
H 10–40cm. An upright or spreading, slender, hairless herb with long-stalked, rounded leaves at the base, and narrow stem leaves. Flowers pale blue, drooping bells. Fl 7–9; H, Pa; P.

GENERAL FEATURES

The bellflowers are mainly a distinctive family, with large, usually blue, bell-like flowers in spikes or clusters. Their leaves are arranged alternately, unlike the very similar gentians, which have opposite leaves. The leaves themselves are undivided and without stipules. The scabiouses, valerians and teasels have tiny flowers in dense, colourful heads.

HABITATS

Harebell and clustered bellflower are both plants of open, dry grassland; harebell grows on acid soil or grassland with soil rich in lime, while clustered bellflower only grows in limey soils. Other bellflower species are most commonly found in woods and along woodland edges and roadsides.

Devilsbit scabious (but no other type of scabious) is the caterpillar food-plant for the beautiful, uncommon marsh fritillary butterfly. The caterpillars are black and bristly, and feed openly in large numbers on the plants in summer, so they are easy to spot. The butterflies fly in June.

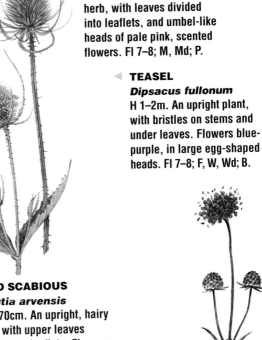

COMMON VALERIAN
Valeriana officinalis
H 30–130cm. A tall, graceful herb, with leaves divided into leaflets, and umbel-like heads of pale pink, scented flowers. Fl 7–8; M, Md; P.

CLUSTERED BELLFLOWER
Campanula glomerata
H 10–30cm. An upright, hairy herb, with oval leaves. Flowers blue, in dense heads at the tops of the stems. Fl 7–8; Md, Pa; P.

TEASEL
Dipsacus fullonum
H 1–2m. An upright plant, with bristles on stems and under leaves. Flowers blue-purple, in large egg-shaped heads. Fl 7–8; F, W, Wd; B.

FIELD SCABIOUS
Knautia arvensis
H 30–70cm. An upright, hairy plant, with upper leaves divided into leaflets. Flowers bluish-pink, in rounded heads. Fl 7–9; Md, Pa; P.

DEVILSBIT SCABIOUS
Succisa pratensis
H 20–60cm. An upright herb, with undivided, almost untoothed leaves and mauve-blue flower heads. Fl 8–10; M, Wd, Md, Pa; P.

THE DAISY FAMILY 1

HEMP AGRIMONY
Eupatorium cannabinum
H 50–120cm. A tall, upright, hairy herb. Leaves mainly 3-lobed, with narrow, pointed, toothed lobes. Small groups of pink flowers, massed together into loose heads. Fl 7–9; M, Wd, M, Pa; P.

GENERAL FEATURES

The daisy family, or composites, are the world's largest family of flowering plants, with at least 14,000 species worldwide. There are hundreds of species in Britain and North Europe alone, so even in 10 pages, we have only been able to make a modest selection. The distinctive features of this family are given overleaf, on p.110.

HABITATS

All of the species shown here are species of open, grassy areas. Daisies are well-known as lawn plants, while yarrow and golden rod are common in a variety of areas with taller grass. Hemp agrimony and fleabane both grow best in damp, flat areas such as fens.

Natural insecticides
Fleabane was once used as a way of getting rid of fleas from bedding – this is what the name 'fleabane' means. Many wild plants have strong odours that can repel certain insects, and often their name reflects this, such as lousewort. A few plants even contain chemicals that can kill insects, and extracts from them have been used as natural insecticides.

YARROW
Achillea millefolium
H 10–40cm. A tufted, hairy herb, with upright, flowering stems and strongly-scented, ferny leaves. Flowers white, creamy, or pink, in large, flat-topped heads. Fl 7–10; F, W, Md, Pa; P.

DAISY
Bellis perennis
H to 12cm. A low herb, with a rosette of spoon-shaped, slightly-toothed leaves. Single flowers on leafless stalks, with white rays and yellow centres. Fl 4–11; F, W, Md, Pa; P.

GOLDEN ROD
Solidago virgaurea
H 10–70cm. An upright herb, with stalked, oval leaves at the base and stalkless stem leaves. Flowers golden-yellow, usually in spikes. Fl 7–9; Mt, Wd, Md, Pa; P.

PROJECT

Hemp agrimony and fleabane are two of the best flowers for attracting insects. Find a clump in calm, sunny weather and watch the insects that visit. Without actually identifying the insects, try to work out which ones are dominant, and which are readily frightened away. It is not necessarily the largest insect species that dominate.

COMMON FLEABANE
Pulicaria dysenterica
H 20–60cm. A hairy, creeping herb, with upright stems. Leaves alternate, oval, toothed. Flowers 2–3cm across, with golden rays and yellow centre. Fl 7–9; M, Wd, Md, Pa; P.

THE DAISY FAMILY 2

GENERAL FEATURES

The daisy family all have one particular feature in common – their 'flowers' are actually made up of large numbers of tiny flowers, or florets. Each flower head has a flattish disc, on which the florets sit. These can be of two main types – small, regular, tube-shaped florets, in which the petals are barely visible; and ray florets, in which the petal tube is extended into a long, strap-shaped petal, toothed at the tip. Some species, such as tansy, have only the tube-shaped florets, whilst other species have a central area of disc florets, and an outer ring of ray florets, such as daisies, or mayweed.

There are two mayweeds that look very similar to scentless mayweed. Scented mayweed has a strong smell; sea mayweed (above) is slightly scented; scentless mayweed is, as its name suggests, scentless.

OX-EYE DAISY
Leucanthemum vulgare
H 20–70cm. An upright, often unbranched herb, with a rosette of spoon-shaped leaves and clasping, toothed stem leaves. Flowers about 3–5cm across, with yellow disc and white rays. Fl 5–8; F, Md, Pa; P.

SCENTLESS MAYWEED ▼
Matricaria perforata
H 10–50cm. A sprawling or semi-upright herb, with feathery, hairless leaves. Flowers 2–4cm across, with yellow disc and white rays. Fl 5–8; F, W, Pa; A or P.

TANSY ▼
Tanacetum vulgare
H 30–100cm. An upright, or occasionally spreading, herb, with strong-smelling leaves. Flowers in numerous, yellow, button-like heads, without rays, each about 1cm across. Fl 7–10; F, W, Md; P.

PINEAPPLEWEED ▲
Chamomilla suaveolens
H 10–25cm. An upright herb, with leaves smelling strongly of pineapple. Green, dome-shaped flowers. Fl 6–10; F, W; A.

HOW TO FIND

Corn marigold was once a common weed of arable fields, but is now becoming rare. It has greyish, toothed leaves, and flowers that have an orange disc and orange rays, about 4–6cm across. The best place to find it is around the edges of fields of crops, on acid, and especially sandy, soil. It does well in areas where the farming is not too intensive.

THE DAISY FAMILY 3

LESSER BURDOCK
Arctium minus
H 60–130cm. An upright,
buchy plant, with woolly
stems. Leaves at the base
are large, up to 40cm long,
and almost as wide, with
smaller leaves up the stem.
Flower heads oval, with
greenish bracts and purple
florets. Fl 7–9; F, W, Wd; P.

GENERAL FEATURES

All the flowers on this spread share the general
features of the composite family, although some
look a little unusual. Burdock has heads of disc
florets, but the bracts surrounding them are
large and hooked, dwarfing the area of flowers,
and making the familiar 'bur' or 'stickyjack' that
sticks to clothing. In butterbur, the heads of
florets are massed together into a spike, and
male and female flowers are on separate plants.

HABITATS

The species shown here are all plants of
disturbed or waste ground, with the exception of
butterbur, which grows alongside rivers.
Ragwort is quite a serious weed, because it is
also poisonous.

a   **b**

There is another species of
burdock – greater burdock –
which looks very similar to
lesser burdock. One way to
tell them apart is by
comparing their lower
leaves. Greater burdock (a)
has blunt leaves which are
as wide as they are long,
while lesser burdock's
leaves (b) are pointed and
narrower.

RAGWORT
Senecio jacobaea
H 30–100cm. An upright, almost hairless herb, with rosettes of crinkly leaves. Flowers with orange discs and paler yellow rays, in branched heads. Poisonous. Fl 6–12; F, W, Pa; B.

BUTTERBUR
Petasites hybridus
H 10–40cm (females in seed much taller). Leaves rounded, very large; produced after the spikes of numerous pinkish heads of flowers. Seeds white and feathery. Fl 3–5; M, Md; P.

GROUNDSEL
Senecio vulgaris
H 10–40cm..A weakly upright, slightly hairy herb, with blunt-lobed leaves. Flowers in small heads, 4–5mm across, with yellow disc florets and few ray florets. Fl all year; F, W; A.

COLTSFOOT
Tussilago farfara
H 5–20cm. Yellow flowers with narrow ray florets. Flowers are produced on thick stems with scale leaves only, before main, triangular leaves. Fl 3–4; F, W, Pa; P.

THE DAISY FAMILY 4

SPEAR THISTLE
Cirsium vulgare
H 40–150cm. An upright, branched plant, with prickly stems. Leaves lobed and spiny, with a long, thick spike at the end. Flower heads large, to 3cm wide, purple. Fl 7–10; F, W; B.

GENERAL FEATURES

The term 'thistle' does not have a very strict meaning, but it basically includes the various members of the daisy family that have spiny leaves and tight heads of rayless flowers, which are usually pink or purple. Knapweeds are very close relatives of thistles, although they are not generally spiny.

HABITATS

Thistles are well known as weeds, and many species of thistle do grow best on cultivated land, where they compete with crops. Spear thistle and creeping thistle are particularly fierce competitors. Knapweed, however, is a plant of roadsides and meadows, whilst marsh thistle prefers damp grassland.

There is one species of thistle, known as the stemless thistle, that ought to be called the picnic thistle. It has very spiny, flat rosettes of leaves, and grows well on dry, sunny banks and cliff tops. In such places, wherever you sit or put your hand, a thistle is waiting.

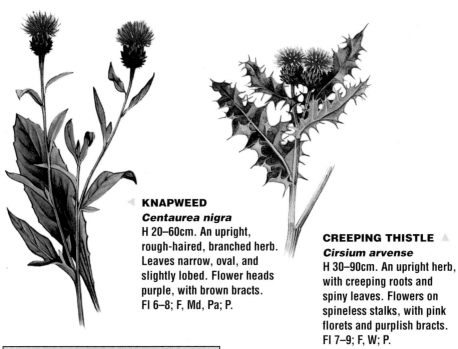

KNAPWEED
Centaurea nigra
H 20–60cm. An upright, rough-haired, branched herb. Leaves narrow, oval, and slightly lobed. Flower heads purple, with brown bracts. Fl 6–8; F, Md, Pa; P.

CREEPING THISTLE
Cirsium arvense
H 30–90cm. An upright herb, with creeping roots and spiny leaves. Flowers on spineless stalks, with pink florets and purplish bracts. Fl 7–9; F, W; P.

PROJECT

Creeping thistles are often attacked by a fly that causes a large, round growth, called a gall, on the stem. Many other plants suffer from galls, such as Robin's pincushion on rose, and oak apple on oak. Try collecting good examples of a few galls in late summer, and keep them in a container so that you can see what the gall-forming insects look like.

MARSH THISTLE
Cirsium palustre
H 40–150cm. An upright, slender plant with a spiny stem. Flowers dark red-purple, (sometimes white), in clusters of small heads. Fl 7–9; M, Md, Pa; B.

THE DAISY FAMILY 5

GENERAL FEATURES

The plants shown here share the same general features as the rest of the daisy family. They all have yellow flowers, and most have hollow stems which ooze a milky fluid when cut. Dandelions have single flower heads on leafless, hollow stems, while the sow-thistles have branched, leafy clusters of flowers.

HABITATS

Dandelions and most sow-thistles are plants of waste ground, cultivated land and generally disturbed places. Although dandelions grow in more closed grassland, a field that is full of dandelions has almost certainly been ploughed a year or two before. Mouse-ear hawkweed grows best in dry grasslands.

Dandelions come in a bewildering variety of forms. They have a strange method of reproduction, in which the flowers produce seeds without being fertilised by pollen. The result is that literally hundreds of very similar species now exist, to which scientists have given different names. They are very hard to identify.

DANDELION
Taraxacum officinalis
H 5–20cm. Herb, with a rosette of deeply toothed or cut leaves. Flower heads large, deep yellow, with up to 200 strap-shaped florets, on thick, hollow, leafless stalks. Fl 3–10; Mt, M, F, W, Md, Pa; P.

CORN SOW-THISTLE
Sonchus arvensis
H 60–150cm. A tall, upright herb. Upper parts of stem covered with yellow hairs. Flowers large, yellow, 4–5cm across, in branched heads. Fl 7–10; F, W; P.

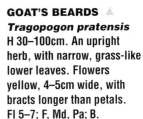

GOAT'S BEARDS
Tragopogon pratensis
H 30–100cm. An upright herb, with narrow, grass-like lower leaves. Flowers yellow, 4–5cm wide, with bracts longer than petals. Fl 5–7; F, Md, Pa; B.

MOUSE-EAR HAWKWEED
Hieracium pilosella
H to 30cm. Herb with rosette of leaves and yellow flowers. Fl 5–8; H, Md, Pa; P.

PROJECT

All the plants shown here have seeds with parachute-like extensions to allow them to blow around in the wind. Dandelion 'clocks' are especially familiar. Find some of these plants in seed, and watch them on a windy day. As the seeds break away, try following them to see where they land. How far do the furthest go, or do you lose them altogether? This demonstrates how plants like these find new, suitable sites in which to grow.

LILY FAMILY AND RELATIVES

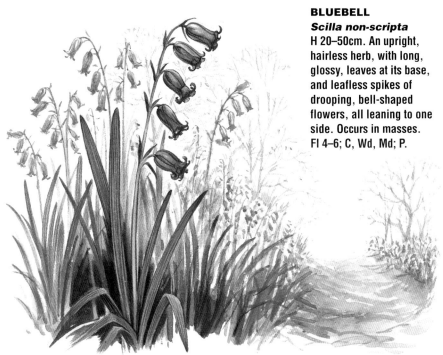

BLUEBELL
Scilla non-scripta
H 20–50cm. An upright, hairless herb, with long, glossy, leaves at its base, and leafless spikes of drooping, bell-shaped flowers, all leaning to one side. Occurs in masses. Fl 4–6; C, Wd, Md; P.

GENERAL FEATURES

All flowering plants belong to one or other of two groups – the monocotyledons and the dicotyledons. The plants shown here, and those on pp.120–123, (unlike the rest of the plants in this book) are all monocotyledons. The leaves of monocotyledons have parallel veins running from top to bottom. Their flower parts are usually in multiples of three – for example, three petals, six stamens etc. When the seed of a monocotyledon starts to grow, it produces a single leaf, rather than a pair of leaves as in dicotyledons. The best-represented monocotyledon family from northern Europe, apart from grasses, is the lily family. Many members of the lily family, and most monocotyledons, produce underground bulbs or corms to enable them to survive the winter.

There are several other species of garlic, as well as wild garlic. A number of these replace their normal flowers with tiny bulbs; these are not seeds, because they are not the result of fertilisation, but they do produce new garlic plants.

118

FLOWERING RUSH
Butomus umbellatus
H 50–150cm. An upright,
rooted, water plant, with
long, grass-like leaves.
Flowers pink, 2–3cm across,
in large, irregular umbels.
Fl 7–9; M, R; P.

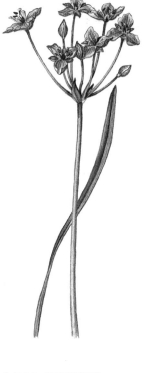

WILD GARLIC
Allium ursinum
H 10–25cm. An upright herb,
with two or three, broad,
garlic-scented leaves.
Flowers white, in rounded
umbels of up to 20 flowers,
with papery bracts below.
Fl 4–6; Wd, Pa; P.

BOG ASPHODEL
Narthecium ossifragum
H 10–40cm. An upright,
bulbed plant, with stiff,
narrow leaves, and spikes
of bright yellow flowers
with orange anthers;
turns orange-red in
autumn. Fl 7–8; M; P.

FROGBIT
Hydrocharis morsus-ranae
H floating at water surface. A
water plant, with floating,
kidney-shaped leaves. Its
large, white flowers have
three crinkly petals, each
with a yellow spot at its
base. Fl 7–8; R; P.

MISCELLANEOUS MONOCOTS

GENERAL FEATURES

The flowers shown here all share the same monocotyledon features as mentioned on p.118, but they come from a variety of different families, each with different characteristics. Iris comes from the iris family, lily-of-the-valley and Solomon's seal come from the lily family, black bryony comes from the tropical yam family, and snowdrop and wild daffodil are both in the daffodil family. They differ in such features as the position of the ovary in relation to the stamens, sepals and petals, and in the shape of the petals and sepals, which in iris are particularly distinctive.

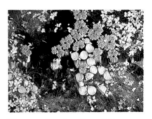

The seeds of yellow iris, which are large, golden brown, and slightly spongy, can float on water. The air spaces within them help to keep them afloat for many months. This is how yellow iris, and many other water or riverside plants, spread to suitable, new locations.

YELLOW IRIS
Iris pseudacorus
H 40–150cm. An upright plant, with large, flattened, sword-shaped leaves, reaching as high as the large, bright yellow flowers.
Fl 5–7; M, R, Pa; P.

SOLOMON'S SEAL ▲
Polygonatum
multiflorum
H 30–80cm. An upright herb, with arching stems and alternate, oval, unstalked, leaves. Flowers greenish-white, in clusters of two to four. Fl 5–6; Wd; P.

BLACK BRYONY ▲
Tamus communis
H to 2–3m on other plants. A scrambling herb with glossy, oval leaves and greenish flowers, producing clusters of glossy, red berries. Fl 5–7; F, Wd; P.

LILY-OF-THE-VALLEY ▲
Convallaria majalis
H 10–20cm. An upright plant, with creeping underground stems. One-sided spikes of drooping, white flowers. Fl 5–6; Wd; P.

◄ SNOWDROP
Galanthus nivalis
H 15–25cm. Famlliar upright herb, with grey-green, narrow leaves and solitary, drooping, white flowers. Fl 2–4; Wd; P.

WILD DAFFODIL ▶
Narcissus
pseudonarcissus
H 20–35cm. Upright herb, with long, narrow leaves. Flowers have pale yellow petals and golden trumpet. Fl 3–4; Wd, Md, Pa; P.

ORCHIDS AND OTHERS

LORDS AND LADIES
Arum maculatum
H 15–30cm. An upright, fleshy herb with large, arrowhead-shaped leaves. Flowers have large, green hood with a purple or yellow spike. Not a member of the orchid family. Fl 4-5; Wd, F; P.

GENERAL FEATURES

Orchids are among the most exotic and exciting of our native plants. They are usually quite recognisable from a distance by their conspicuous spikes of flowers, often standing out from other vegetation. In close-up, their flowers are extraordinary, with three outer sepals and three inner petals. Many of the common names of orchids, such as bee orchid, fly orchid or lizard orchid, are based on the peculiar, sometimes animal-like, shapes of the lowest of the flower petals.

HABITATS

Although orchids do occur everywhere, most of them grow on chalk or limestone soil, often on downs or in woodland.

This small elephant hawk moth has visited the flowers of a butterfly orchid during the night for its nectar, and has picked up two yellow pollen masses on its head. The insect will almost certainly pollinate the next butterfly orchid flower it visits.

WHITE HELLEBORINE ▲
Cephelanthera damasonium
H 15-50cm. Upright, hairless plant, with long, oval leaves. Vase-shaped flowers dull white with orange blotch inside. Fl 6–7; Wd, Pa; P.

BIRD'S NEST ORCHID ▲
Neottia nidus-avis
H 20–40cm. A pale yellow-brown plant, with no green colouring at all, and brown flowers. Lives on rotting leaves. Fl 5–7; Wd; P.

COMMON TWAYBLADE ▲
Listera ovata
H 20–65cm. Dull green plant, with pair of oval leaves near base of stem. Flowers greenish-yellow, in thin spikes. Fl 6–7; Wd, Md, Pa; P.

PROJECT

Try marking out a small area of ground where orchids are growing. The best place is in a nature reserve, but remember to ask permission first. Draw out a grid, then record the number and the positions of all the flowering plants. If you check the same area again each year, you will soon get a good idea of how long orchids live and how often they flower.

SOUTHERN MARSH ORCHID ▲
Dactylorhiza praetermissa
H 20–60cm. An upright plant, with a fleshy, hollow stem, and broad, pointed leaves. Pinkish flowers in a dense spike. Fl 6–7; M, Md; P.

123

ORCHIDS 2

GENERAL FEATURES

Early purple orchid and common spotted orchid are among the commonest and most widespread of our native orchids. Both have spotted leaves and upright cylindrical spikes of flowers, although the early purple orchid generally flowers earlier, has glossier leaves, and redder flowers than spotted orchid.

As well as looking very like small bees, the flowers of bee orchids actually produce a female bee 'smell'. They are therefore highly attractive to male bees, which will even attempt to mate with a flower. In doing so, the pollen masses of the orchid flower stick to the insect's body, to be carried on to another flower.

HABITATS

The early purple orchid can be found almost everywhere, from shady woodlands, to grasslands and even high on mountains. Spotted orchid is almost as widespread, growing in both shade and sunshine, while butterfly orchid grows in similar places but is less common. Bee orchid and pyramidal orchid are generally confined to chalky grasslands.

EARLY PURPLE ORCHID
Orchis mascula
H 30cm. Upright plant with purple-red, spotted flowers in a loose spike. Leaves glossy, with dark purple spots. Fl 4–6; Wd, Md, Mt; P.

COMMON SPOTTED ORCHID
Dactylorhiza fuchsii
H 40cm. Flowers pinkish with darker, red markings. Rosette of grey-green, spotted leaves at the base of the stems. Fl 6–7; Wd, Md; M; P.

GREATER BUTTERFLY ORCHID
Platanthera chlorantha
H 40cm. Upright plant, with single stem bearing fragrant, creamy-white flowers. Along with the lesser butterfly orchid, it is protected by law in many countries. Fl 5–7; Wd, Md; P.

PYRAMIDAL ORCHID
Anacamptis pyramidalis
H 30cm. Pyramid-shaped, pink flower heads with a distinctive 'foxy' smell. Narrow, pointed, unspotted leaves. Fl 6–8; Md, Pa, C; P.

BEE ORCHID
Ophrys apifera
H 25cm. So-called because each flower appears to have a bee resting on it. Uncommon. Leaves oval, unspotted, getting smaller up the stem. Fl 6–7; F, Pa, Md; P.

INDEX

ILLUSTRATIONS BY

(t = top, b = bottom, l = left, r = right, c = centre)

Garden Studios: Roger Gorringe 44, 46, 48, 50, 52, 54, 56, 58, 60, 62, 64, 66, 68, 70, 72, 74, 76, 78, 80, 82, 84, 86, 88, 90, 92, 94, 96, 98, 100, 102, 104, 106, 108, 110, 112, 114, 116, 118, 120, 122; Roger Kent 45c, 45tr, 45bl, 47bl, 47c, 47tr, 48tr, 49tr, 49br, 51cr, 51br, 53tr, 53cr, 54tr, 55tl, 55tc, 55br, 56br, 57br, 59bl, 59tr, 60br, 63br, 69bl, 69br, 71br, 75, 80br, 81br, 83tl, 83tr, 83br, 85tr, 86tr, 87bc, 87cr, 90tr, 91tr, 93tr, 100cr, 105tr, 107tl, 107c, 112cr, 119bl, 119c, 119tr, 121tr, 121br, 123, 125; Josephine Martin 17, 20; Liz Pepperell 5, 6, 7, 18, 19, 22 · Linden Artists: Shirley Felts cover; Gillian Kenny 124; Phil Weare 28/29 · Maltings Partnership 10, 11, 13 · Bernard Thornton Artists: Fred Anderson 24/25, 26/27, 30/31, 32/33, 34/35, 36/37, 38/39, 40/41, 42/43; Bob Bampton 8, 9, 21. Additional black and white line illustrations by Linden Artists. All other illustrations from *Hamlyn's Guide to British Wild Flowers* and *Edible and Medicinal Plants of Britain and Northern Europe*.

The publishers would like to thank the following organisations and individuals for their kind permission to reproduce the photographs in this book:

Stephen Gorton 23br, 82.

All other photographs supplied by Natural Image (Bob and Liz Gibbons).